Free-Motion Quilting Made Easy

Free-Motion Quilting Made Easy

186 DESIGNS from
8 SIMPLE SHAPES

Eva A. Larkin

Martingale®
& COMPANY

Dedication

To God, who truly makes all things possible.

Acknowledgments

I can't begin to thank all the friends, students, customers, and quilt shop owners who walked with me along this journey. Your trust and support kept me moving toward the goal of writing and finishing this book. I am so blessed to have you all in my life.

I also have to acknowledge my official book "think tank," my cats, Elizabeth and Abigail. They were with me every step of the way, Elizabeth on my lap and Abigail in her basket. Where would we be in life without our furry friends?

Free-Motion Quilting Made Easy:
186 Designs from 8 Simple Shapes
© 2009 by Eva A. Larkin

That Patchwork Place® is an imprint
of Martingale & Company®.

Martingale & Company
20205 144th Ave. NE
Woodinville, WA 98072-8478 USA
www.martingale-pub.com

Printed in China
13 12 11 10 09   8 7 6 5 4 3

Library of Congress Cataloging-in-Publication Data
Library of Congress Control Number: 2008045657

ISBN: 978-1-56477-882-6

Mission Statement

*Dedicated to providing quality products
and service to inspire creativity.*

Credits

President & CEO • Tom Wierzbicki

Editorial Director • Mary V. Green

Managing Editor • Tina Cook

Developmental Editor • Karen Costello Soltys

Technical Editor • Ellen Pahl

Copy Editor • Marcy Heffernan

Design Director • Stan Green

Production Manager • Regina Girard

Illustrator • Laurel Strand

Cover & Text Designer • Regina Girard

Photographer • Brent Kane

Contents

Introduction

In 2003, I slowly developed a small quilting business using my domestic sewing machine instead of a long-arm quilting machine. As my business grew, I found it a constant challenge to find new and interesting designs that I could successfully quilt on my machine. I wanted designs that didn't need to be marked and weren't just allover meandering designs.

About a year later I started teaching free-motion quilting and discovered that my students were struggling with these same issues. They loved the idea of easy block-based designs that could be accomplished without hours of practice. I started playing with design ideas that I could use in my own work and teach my students as well. A class evolved and was a hit. It was fantastic to see the students come away from the class confident and inspired. They were proof that the ideas and designs worked. It was due to their encouragement that I decided to put the designs into a book.

I also discovered during my classes that the reason so many quilters are uncomfortable with free-motion quilting is that they feel out of control with their technique. They don't know how to achieve and maintain consistent results in their stitching. I have identified three areas on which to focus as a tangible way to improve your skills: mastering stitch tension, controlling stitch length, and quilting in smaller sections. These focus areas are covered more fully in "Free-Motion Quilting Basics" on page 9. They ultimately take the guesswork out of free-motion quilting. I always start my classes by reviewing them and have written this book following the same format, with exercises for you to practice what you learn.

> I found it a constant challenge to find new and interesting quilting designs.

The quilting designs, all derived from eight basic shapes, are truly the backbone of this book. Each shape can be used to create at least five designs. The key aspect is the ease with which each shape and design can be controlled when quilted. The result is great-looking quilting without hours of practice or time spent marking the quilt. I also combine the eight basic shapes in various ways to produce more than 186 quilting patterns. The designs are organized so you can easily find and work with the combinations of your favorite shapes. This allows you to focus on designs you know you can successfully quilt.

In addition I've included a chapter to guide you in deciding how to quilt your quilt. I've made the process systematic, giving you a method to follow whenever you have a finished quilt top. I've also provided plenty of design inspiration and a gallery to give you even more ideas for using the designs. The possibilities are truly endless.

The final chapter is a troubleshooting guide that provides answers to common problems that come up while free-motion quilting. It should help you to quickly resolve the problem and get back to your quilting.

The information and easy designs in this book will provide you with a free-motion method that produces consistent, good-looking results. It puts you, the quilter, back in control. It is my hope that this book will excite you and make you eager to free-motion quilt all those wonderful tops waiting to become fabulous quilts!

Getting Started

The following list outlines the supplies and preparations needed for free-motion quilting. Please take a moment to review them and prepare your sewing machine before beginning.

What You'll Need Checklist

- Recently cleaned and serviced sewing machine and sewing machine manual
- Sewing machine extension table (optional, but highly recommended)
- Free-motion quilting (darning) foot
- Machine-quilting thread. You'll have fewer problems with thread breakage and a lot less lint in the bobbin if you use a high-quality thread. My personal favorite is Signature machine-quilting thread. It's 100%-mercerized long-staple cotton and is a 3-ply/40-weight thread. I use this for both the top thread and the bobbin.
- New quilting needle. Quilting needles are stronger than normal sewing needles, and you'll be less likely to break one of these when free-motion quilting. I recommend Schmetz quilting needles, size 90/14.
- 4½" square ruler (optional)
- 1" x 12" clear acrylic ruler
- Fabric-marking pencil or pen. My favorite is a Clover Chaco Liner in white because I know for sure the color will brush out when I'm done. For practice exercises, a regular pen or pencil is fine.
- Quilting gloves (optional). Quilting gloves can be any type of glove that helps you more easily grip and move the fabric with less physical effort. Usually an actual quilting glove will have some type of rubber grips on the fingertip area. My favorites are Machingers because they're made of nylon, making them breathable while still being form fitting.
- Paper and pencil (or pen) for drawing designs

Choosing a Thread Color

I like to decide how I'm going to quilt a finished top before I purchase my thread. This way I know what color fabric I'll actually be quilting on and can get the best thread color to blend with it. It's simply a matter of auditioning the thread on the finished quilt. I do this by unwinding about an arm's length of thread and laying it across the section I'm going to quilt. This shows me the true amount of contrast between the thread and the fabric. Free-motion quilting is never going to be absolutely perfect, and I don't want any "imperfect" spots to be overly obvious. The greater the contrast between the fabric and the thread, the more the stitching shows up. I want the texture of the design to be more noticeable than the thread color.

Unwind the Spool of Thread

Be careful about simply holding a spool of thread up against the quilt top when trying to decide on thread color. The color will appear darker when condensed on the spool. You'll get the best representation of the actual color and how it will look on the quilt by unwinding it and laying it on the completed quilt top.

Choosing Backing Fabric

I suggest that you wait to purchase your backing fabric until after you have decided how you'll quilt your finished top and selected a thread color. Then choose a fabric that matches the thread color. This will help hide any stitch imperfections, and you can use the same color thread in the top of the machine and in the bobbin. Any "moments" of bad stitch tension won't be noticeable.

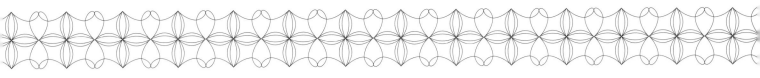

Free-Motion Quilting Basics

Many quilters are uncomfortable with free-motion quilting because they feel out of control with their technique. They just don't know how to achieve and maintain consistent results. I felt the same way when I started. I remember being told that free-motion quilting "just took practice." The problem was I didn't know what to practice. I needed something tangible to work on. Over the years, I have identified three areas you can focus on to improve your skills. I refer to them as the "free-motion basics." They are mastering thread tension, controlling stitch length, and quilting in smaller sections.

In this chapter I'll explain each of the basics in detail and walk you through some quick exercises. You'll be amazed at how quickly you gain confidence in your free-motion quilting ability. I highly recommend reviewing this chapter, regardless of your level of experience. You just might pick up a helpful hint or two along the way.

For the practice exercises, you'll need to make some "fabric sandwiches." A fabric sandwich consists of two pieces of fabric with a layer of batting between them. Make three 12" square fabric sandwiches from scraps of fabric and low-loft (thin) batting. It isn't necessary to pin or baste them for the exercises.

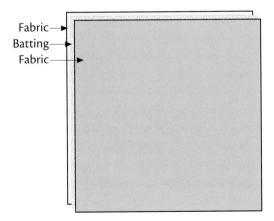

Fabric →
Batting →
Fabric →

Prepare Your Machine Checklist

- *Attach the free-motion quilting (darning) foot in place of the regular presser foot.*
- *Thread the sewing machine with the same quilting thread in both the top and the bobbin.*
- *Drop the feed dogs. When the feed dogs are down, you'll manually move the fabric under the needle. (Check your sewing machine manual if you're not sure how to drop the feed dogs.)*
- *Put in a new quilting needle.*
- *Engage the needle-down function, if available. (Check your sewing machine manual if you're unsure if this is an option on your machine.)*

Thread Tension

Thread tension is the amount of "strength" needed for the top thread to pull the bobbin thread up to its proper position. The thread tension is set correctly when the threads meet in the middle of the two layers of fabric being sewn.

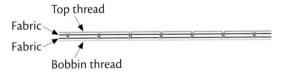

Top thread
Fabric
Fabric
Bobbin thread

Normal thread tension is set for sewing two layers of fabric together. You have to adjust the tension when you machine quilt because of the batting. The top thread tension is no longer strong enough to pull the bobbin thread to its proper position in the batting. The tension is *too loose* and is often the reason why you'll see the bobbin thread left lying across the back of the quilt.

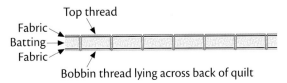

Top thread
Fabric
Batting
Fabric
Bobbin thread lying across back of quilt

Most thread tension problems are fixed by *increasing* the tension. Do this by turning the thread tension dial to a higher number in half-step increments. For example, if a machine's standard thread-tension setting is 4, start by setting the tension halfway between 4 and 5. Sew a test sample. If it still isn't correct, increase the tension by another half step.

You'll know the tension is correct when a "pillowing" effect appears around the thread on both the front and back of the quilt. The pillowing occurs because both the top and bobbin thread are being pulled into the fabric and batting on both sides of the quilt.

Some sewing machines have an "auto-adjust" feature for thread tension. This works great for normal sewing but doesn't always work for machine quilting. Check your manual and make sure you know how to manually adjust the tension if the auto adjustment isn't working correctly.

Tension is correct. *Pillowing occurs around stitches.*

Tension is too loose. *The bobbin thread is lying on the back of the quilt because the top thread is not pulling the bobbin thread into the fabric and the batting.* ***Tighten*** *the tension by* ***increasing*** *the thread tension number.*

Tension is too tight. *The bobbin thread pops to the top of the quilt, as shown by the red thread dots. Loosen the tension by decreasing the thread tension number.*

Thread Tension Exercise

Testing the thread tension before you start to quilt will help ensure beautiful results. Follow the steps below each time you start a new project. The tension setting that works for one quilt will not necessarily work for the next. Changes in fabric weight, batting thickness, and type of thread used can all affect the tension. Read through "Getting Started" on page 8 and follow the checklist on page 9 to prepare your machine. When doing a tension sample before quilting a specific quilt, be sure to make your fabric sandwich from the same fabric and batting that will be used in the quilt.

1. Lower the feed dogs and place the fabric sandwich under the needle so that you'll be sewing along its right or left side. Lower the presser foot and turn the machine flywheel by hand to insert the needle down into the fabric sandwich.

2. Holding the fabric sandwich so you can move it easily, start sewing and moving the fabric away from yourself at a steady pace. Remember, once the feed dogs are dropped, the sewing machine's stitch-length function is no longer engaged. If you don't move the fabric, it won't go anywhere! Sew until your line of stitches is 3" to 4" long.

3. Raise the presser foot, turn the flywheel to raise the needle from the fabric, clip the threads, and take the fabric sandwich out from under the needle.

4. Check the thread tension on both the front and back of the fabric sandwich. If the stitches are too small to see clearly, sew another line of stitches with the machine running slower.

5. Look for the pillowing effect around the stitches on both sides of the fabric sandwich. If it's not there, adjust the tension by a half-step increment and sew another line of stitches. Continue testing until it's correct. Remember, in most cases the tension is too loose and needs to be tightened.

Monitor the Tension

The thread tension on a sewing machine is fairly sensitive. You can easily pull it out of alignment by moving or pulling the quilt too quickly. Therefore, develop the habit of regularly checking your thread tension on the back of the quilt about every 15 to 30 minutes. I don't cut my threads or take the quilt out from under the machine. I just flip it over and look at the area closest to the needle to make sure the bobbin thread isn't lying on the back of the quilt and that the thread isn't pulling around the corners of the design. If you notice a problem, adjust the tension and test it on your fabric sandwich before resuming the quilting on your quilt.

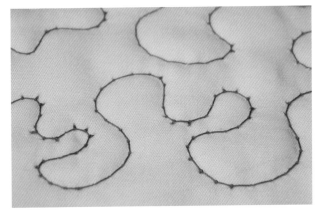

Tension is out of alignment. *Tighten the tension to eliminate pulling around curves and corners of a design.*

Pull, Secure, and Trim

There are three very important things you need to do each time you begin free-motion quilting or after you've cut your threads and have moved to a new area: *pull, secure, and trim.* I like to think of it like the phrase, "stop, drop, and roll." (Remember learning that as a child in case you caught on fire?)

Pull the bobbin thread up to the top of the quilt. This prevents the thread from getting caught in the stitches on the back of the quilt and making a "thread nest" that's almost impossible to cut out.

Secure the threads by taking a few tiny stitches forward and back. This prevents the stitches from coming undone.

Trim threads as close to the fabric as possible. Trimming ensures that the long thread tails won't get in the way as you quilt, and you won't have to go back later to trim them.

1. *Pull* the bobbin thread to the top of the quilt by first lowering the free-motion foot. Then hold the top thread with your left hand and keep a little tension on it. Lower and raise the needle using either your needle up/down function or by turning your flywheel

one complete turn. The bobbin thread should come up as a loop caught on the top thread. Lift your presser foot lift lever and pull the bobbin thread out more. If the bobbin thread will not come up easily, move the needle to its highest position.

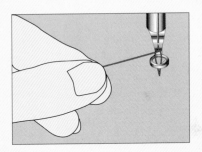

2. Make sure both threads are under the free-motion foot before lowering it. *Secure* your threads by taking a couple of short stitches forward and backward. Remember, you control the movement of the fabric.

3. *Trim* the thread ends.

Auto-Stitch Secure: Some machines will automatically secure or tie your threads for you. This is a great feature if you have it. Check your sewing machine manual to verify if this is an option.

Stitch Length

The desired stitch length for free-motion quilting is about ⅛" or eight stitches per inch. However, unless you have an actual stitch regulator for your sewing machine, it's impossible to make all the stitches exactly the same length. The goal is to have the *majority* of the stitches about ⅛" long.

The feed dogs on a sewing machine are what normally control and regulate stitch length when sewing. Once you drop the feed dogs, you must manually control the stitch length by moving the fabric with your hands and varying the speed of the machine. I've found it much easier to control my stitch length by focusing on the speed of the machine rather than hand movement. I like to think of the foot pedal of the sewing machine like the gas pedal of a car.

- If the majority of stitches are shorter than ⅛", you're moving the quilt too slowly in relation to the speed of the machine. The machine needs to be slowed down—let off the gas.

- If the majority of stitches are longer than ⅛", you're moving the quilt too quickly in relation to the speed of the machine. You'll need to give the machine more gas—speed up.

Slow Down and Take Control

Some quilters believe you have to run the machine as fast as possible when free-motion quilting. This just isn't true. The key is to run the machine at a speed where you feel in control and are able to achieve the desired stitch length of ⅛".

It can be hard to control the stitch length of your first few stitches any time you start to free-motion quilt. Once again, I find it helpful to relate it to driving a car. When you accelerate from a stopped position, you do so by gradually applying pressure to the gas pedal. Do basically the same thing for free-motion quilting. Start by slowly giving the sewing machine some "gas" before you begin moving your hands. Then gradually increase the movement of your hands in correlation to the speed of the machine until the desired stitch length is achieved.

Stitch Length Exercise

In this exercise you'll stitch a spiral. This gives you practice controlling stitch length. Focus on how changing the speed of your machine changes your stitch length. Read through the directions completely before beginning the exercise.

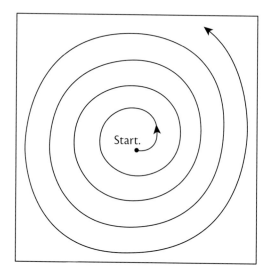

1. Using the same fabric sandwich as you used for testing the thread tension, start in the middle of the fabric sandwich so you have enough fabric to hold onto while doing the exercise. Stitch the spiral by eye; you don't need to mark it. The shape doesn't matter.

2. Slowly start the machine and begin moving your hands in a circular motion to stitch the

spiral. *Don't turn the fabric around in a circle in order to create the spiral design.* Your hands should be making the circular movement. It's like drawing with thread.

3. Stitch a couple of rounds of the spiral, and then stop. Don't worry about how your spiral looks, just focus on your stitches.

4. Check the stitch length. Are the majority of the stitches about ⅛" long? Check them with a ruler if you're unsure.

5. Decide whether the stitch length needs to be adjusted. If the *majority* of stitches are too small, slow down the speed of your machine. If the *majority* of stitches are too long, speed up your machine.

6. Stitch another couple of rounds on the spiral and check the stitch length again. Continue stitching until you achieve the desired stitch length.

7. Flip the fabric sandwich over and check the thread tension. It might have come out of alignment due to the extra movement involved in quilting the spiral. Make any necessary adjustments before continuing to the next exercise. (Refer back to the "Thread Tension Exercise" on page 10 if necessary.)

Help with Stitch Length

Some quilters find it helpful to use the speed control setting on their sewing machines to help maintain a consistent stitch length. The speed control allows you to slow down the speed of the machine to a point where you can maintain the proper stitch length while having the foot pedal completely depressed. Check your sewing machine manual to see if this option is available on your machine. It might be referred to as Half Speed or as Speed Range Control Lever. Give it a try and see if it works for you.

Quilting in Smaller Sections

The last of my three basics for free-motion quilting is learning to quilt in smaller sections. Most domestic sewing machines have an opening that is 5" to 6" wide, which gives you about a 4½"-square area around the needle where there is room to easily move your quilt.

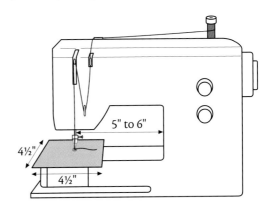

When you can easily move the section of quilt you're working on, you'll have better control of the quilting design, stitch length, and thread tension. By simply focusing on quilting the area under your needle instead of the whole quilt, you'll feel more relaxed and in control because you don't have to push and pull the quilt around to move it, and you'll be less frustrated since you won't be pulling your thread tension out of alignment and having problems with your stitch length.

Two questions often arise when I talk about quilting in smaller sections: What do you do if the block is larger than 4½" square? And how does this rule apply when you want to stipple a whole quilt? The answer is simple, and it's the same for both questions. It's just a matter of breaking the block or quilt into 4½"-square sections and working one section at a time.

For example, if I were going to stipple a quilt, I would start in the center and work out to the sides by quilting one 4½"-square section at a time. You're still quilting the sections continuously. It's just that you change your focus from moving around the whole quilt to working on one small section at a time. In the beginning, you might find it helpful to actually mark the 4½"-square sections on the quilt. I use a white Chaco Liner and mark only a few sections right before I quilt them. I first create a "plus" pattern in the quilt, and then go back and fill in each of the four quadrants.

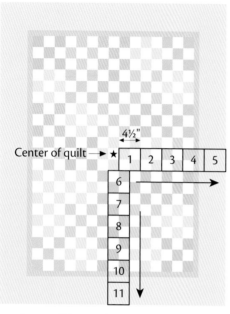

Start quilting in the center of the quilt and work your way out to the edges.

The Quilt Nest

Regardless of the size of the quilt, I can position the quilt to easily move the 4½"-square area that is under the needle. I call this my quilt-nest system, named after watching a swan prepare her nest one day. She sat in the middle of her nest and checked to make sure it was nice and fluffy all the way around her. I decided to try this with a quilt when I was free-motion quilting. By fluffing the quilt around me instead of rolling it to get it under the arm of the machine, I didn't have the weight of the quilt on my body, putting extra stress on my arms and neck. It allowed me to simply focus on the design while easily maintaining control of my free-motion basics.

Here's how to use the quilt-nest system:

1. Make sure there is enough space around the sewing machine for the quilt to lie without catching on something or falling to the floor.

I quilt on an old dining-room table with a light-weight rolling cart pulled to the left side of me. This provides support on all sides of the quilt and allows me to move it easily.

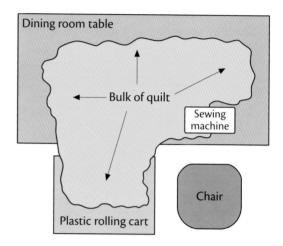

2. Position the area of the quilt to be worked on under the needle.

3. Fluff the quilt and make sure the 4½"-square area under the needle can move easily in all directions. If at any time the quilt becomes hard to move in a certain direction, it's probably caught on something and needs to be re-fluffed.

4. Quilt the 4½"-square section of the quilt that's under the needle.

5. Continue to the next 4½"-square section that needs to be quilted and repeat the fluffing process.

The quilt is spread out on the sewing surface, fluffed, and ready to free-motion quilt using the quilt-nest system.

Frequent Stopping for More Control

You'll feel more relaxed and in control while free-motion quilting if you add frequent stops. Quilting without stopping causes you to feel stressed because you're trying to figure out where to quilt next while still trying to move the quilt around fast enough to keep up with the stitching. You may begin to lose control of your design because you don't know where you're heading next or pull your tension out of alignment because you're moving your quilt too quickly. You may also lose consistency in your stitches because you can't focus on keeping your speed even. You can resolve all of these problems by simply stopping, repositioning the quilt and your hands, and planning where and what to quilt next.

Hand Position

The way you position your hands when free-motion quilting should help you accomplish two things. First, it should keep the fabric under the needle flat and somewhat taut. This gives you a smoother surface that allows you to quilt the design with more ease. It also helps prevent the fabric from bunching and puckering. Second, your hands should also give you enough of a grip on the quilt so that it's easy to move. The hand positions shown at right are ones I frequently use. Note how in each of the examples my hands are within 2" or 3" of the needle. When your hands are farther away you start to lose the ability to control the design. Give each position a try and see which one feels most comfortable for you.

Quilting Gloves

Quilting gloves can make a big difference in your comfort level and control while moving the quilt. They can be gardening gloves, disposable gloves, or actual quilting gloves—any type that improves your grip on the quilt. My favorites are Machingers. I personally cannot quilt without them. While quilting gloves aren't for everyone, I highly recommend giving them a try.

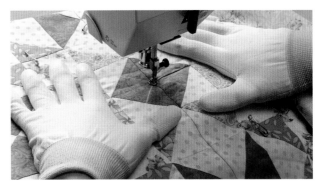

Hands are flat and frame the needle.

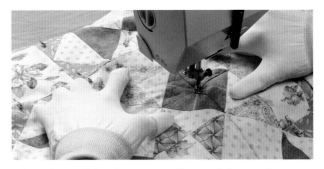

Thumbs and forefingers are flat and frame the needle. The rest of the fingers hold onto the quilt.

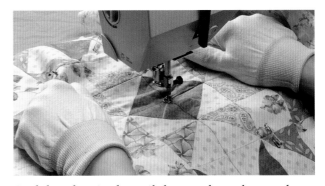

Both hands grip the quilt but are kept close to the needle to frame it.

One hand is kept flat and the other hand grips the quilt. Both are kept close to the needle to frame it.

Putting It All Together—Exercises

You can put into practice what you've learned about the basics of free-motion quilting (mastering thread tension, controlling stitch length, and quilting in smaller sections) with some easy exercises. For most quilters, myself included, the first couple of attempts at free-motion quilting might be a bit rough. Don't give up! You'll become more comfortable, and your stitched designs will become smoother. The best thing to do in the beginning is to pay more attention to learning the basics and less time worrying about the designs!

I've found that if I first become comfortable drawing a design on paper, it's a lot easier for me to quilt. I usually sketch it out until I feel like I can draw it with some consistency; sometimes it takes three to five sketches before I'm ready to quilt a particular design. Drawing the design on paper first will also help you figure out where in the design you can stop and reposition your hands if needed. Try drawing out each of the exercises before quilting them and see if it helps you as well.

Warm Up First

Always do a quick warm-up exercise (like the spiral exercise you used for practicing your stitch length) before starting on a quilt. This gets you limbered up and ready to go.

Exercise 1—Standard Wavy Line

1. Read through the directions before beginning and prepare your sewing machine if you've not already done so. (Refer to the "Prepare Your Machine Checklist" on page 9.)

2. Draw three 4½" squares on both your paper and on a new fabric sandwich. Make sure you draw the practice squares on your fabric sandwich close to the center so you have room to hold on around the edges of the sandwich when quilting. Divide each 4½" square into four sections. You will use this fabric sandwich for all three exercises.

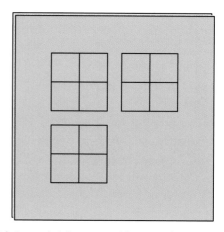

Fabric sandwich prepared for wavy line exercises

3. Practice drawing wavy lines on paper, as shown, until you're comfortable with the design.

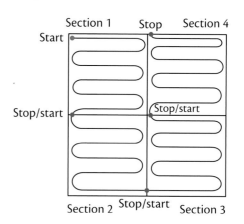

4. When you're ready to sew, make sure your hands frame the needle and have a good grip on the fabric sandwich.

5. Pull, secure, and trim your threads; then slowly start stitching. Quilt a wavy line down section 1 and stop before continuing into section 2. Make sure the needle is down and the machine is completely stopped before removing your hands.

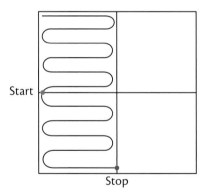

6. Quilt to the bottom of section 2, stopping at section 3.

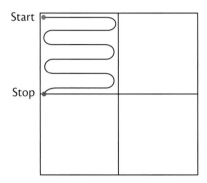

7. Quilt section 3 moving up toward section 4. Be prepared for it to feel a bit strange the first couple of times you quilt "away" from yourself. Stop when you get to the bottom of section 4.

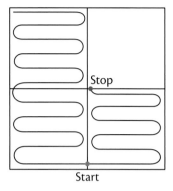

8. Quilt section 4 in the same manner. Secure and trim your threads.

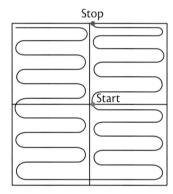

9. Check the thread tension. It might need to be increased or tightened due to the increased movement of your hands. Remember, make only half-step adjustments to thread tension at a time.

10. Check the stitch length. Look to see what the majority of the stitches measure. If the majority of stitches are either longer or shorter than ⅛", redo the exercise, focusing on the stitch length.

Practice Stopping

Did you practice stopping in each of the indicated spots when completing the exercise? If not, try the exercise again putting in the indicated stops. It really does make things easier.

Exercise 2—
Variable Width Wavy Line

1. Practice drawing the variable width wavy line on paper as shown below. Pay attention to where the stops and starts are.

2. Move to the next 4½" square on your fabric sandwich. Pull, secure, and trim the threads. Make sure your hands are framing the needle and you can easily move the fabric sandwich.

3. Slowly start the machine, begin quilting a close wavy line down section 1, and stop before continuing into section 2. Check the length of your stitches. It's not unusual for them to be a bit small. It happens because we are concentrating on quilting the close wavy lines and end up slowing down our hands. Correct it by slowing down the machine until you're more comfortable quilting the close lines.

4. Quilt to the bottom of section 2, stopping beside section 3.

5. Now for the wide wavy lines. It takes a bit more control for the wider design, and most people find their stitch length is too long. Just give it a bit more gas! Quilt a wide wavy line up section 3 moving toward section 4, quilting away from yourself. Stop when you get to the bottom of section 4. How did it go? If you had trouble, you might want to try a different hand position and see if that helps.

6. Quilt section 4 in the same manner. Secure and trim the threads. Check the thread tension and make any necessary corrections.

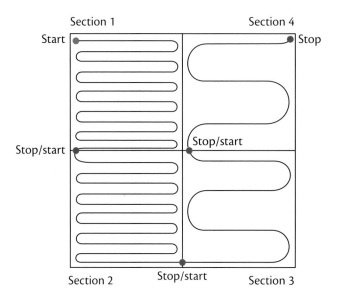

Exercise 3— Changing Direction Wavy Line

1. Draw the wavy line on paper as shown. Pay attention to the stops and starts.

2. Move to the last 4½" square on your fabric sandwich. Pull, secure, and trim your threads. Check your hand position.

3. Slowly start the machine, begin quilting a horizontal wavy line down section 1, and stop before continuing into section 2.

4. Quilt a vertical wavy line to the bottom of section 2, stopping beside section 3. There is nothing to be concerned about if it's a little harder for you to change your quilting direction. Getting used to doing this just takes time.

5. Quilt a horizontal wavy line up section 3 moving toward section 4. Stop when you get to the bottom of section 4.

6. Quilt a vertical wavy line up section 4. Secure and trim your threads, and then check your thread tension and stitch length.

Don't Slide Your Hands

Don't try to reposition your hands while you're quilting by sliding them to the next area. Get in the habit of stopping the machine, and then moving your hands.

Check Your Progress

After you've completed all three exercises, compare your first exercise with your last. Notice how your wavy lines are starting to get a bit smoother. They may not be perfect, but they are getting better. Relax for a few minutes with a cup of coffee or tea, and then draw one more 4½" square on your fabric sandwich and try the first exercise again. You will be amazed at how much easier it is to do!

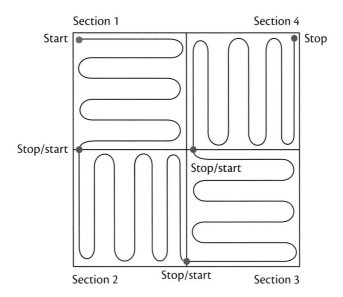

From Simple Shapes to Stunning Designs

Once you know the basics of free-motion quilting (mastering thread tension, controlling stitch length, and quilting in smaller sections) you're ready to move on to the fun part—the quilting designs. A good quilting design doesn't have to be complicated or intricate in order to be effective. My favorite designs are those that are easy to quilt, add texture to the quilt top, and require little marking. The designs in this book meet those requirements.

Eight Basic Shapes

I rely on the eight basic shapes shown below for all my designs. The key element lies in their simplicity. These are shapes that anyone can easily draw. And if you can draw the shape, then you can quilt it. You don't have to be able to draw all of these shapes in order to have lots of design choices. One shape alone offers five different design options.

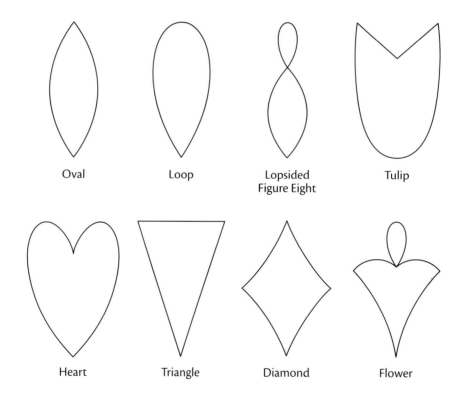

Oval   Loop   Lopsided Figure Eight   Tulip

Heart   Triangle   Diamond   Flower

Take a few minutes and try drawing each of the shapes. Remember, I'm not talking about perfection. Just try them and get comfortable with them.

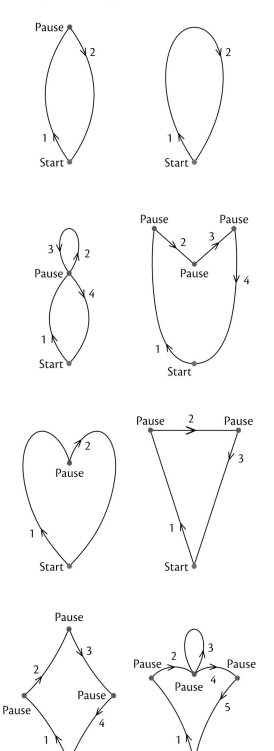

Using Reference Lines

You create the quilting designs by simply repeating the different shapes in the 4½"-square quilting area. It's easier to draw the designs and keep the shapes consistent when you mark the square with horizontal, vertical, and diagonal lines.

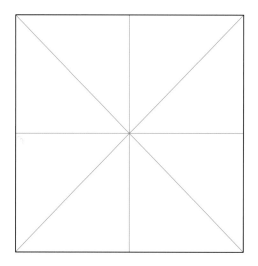

These lines and any points that you mark along them will make quilting the designs easier. They will give your eye a place to focus. Looking *ahead* to where you'll be quilting makes it easier to control the design and keep it more consistent than if you're focused on the needle. The lines and points also provide places to stop while quilting. Each time you stop, you can adjust your grip, ensuring you have the best hand position for completing the design smoothly. I usually mark just one block at a time with the white Chaco Liner.

Mark reference lines and points for each block right before you quilt it.

If You Can Draw It, You Can Quilt It

The best way to get comfortable with each of the designs is to draw them out by hand a few times, following the directions below. You might not be as comfortable with some of the shapes and designs as others. Don't worry! Just try drawing and quilting each one, and then move on. I guarantee you'll find a couple you really like, and those are the ones you can focus on later.

For each of the designs, follow these general instructions:

- Draw a 4½" square on your paper and divide it into four sections with a horizontal and vertical line. Draw in the diagonal lines if they're shown in the diagram.

- Trace the design with your finger following the numbers. Notice how the first two shapes are drawn using a figure-eight motion. I've found drawing it in this manner helps keep the design smoother.

- Draw the design, beginning at the green dot and following the numbered sequence.

- Keep your eyes focused on where you're headed instead of looking at the exact spot you're drawing. This forward focus helps to keep the design smooth and consistent.

- Slow down as you return to the center of the square for each design. This will help you control the crossover of lines in the middle of the design.

- Use the horizontal, vertical, and/or diagonal lines as reference points for keeping the shapes consistent in size.

- Solid red dots in the designs indicate focus points as well as stopping points where you can pause to reposition your hands and make other adjustments as needed.

- Sometimes the instructions will tell you to "travel" on the drawn reference lines. This simply means that you can use the lines as a guide for part of your design for a short distance.

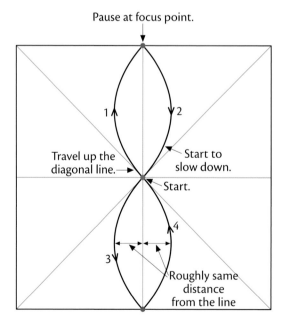

Pause at focus point.

1   2

Travel up the diagonal line. → Start to slow down.

Start.

4

3

Roughly same distance from the line

Practice Quilting

Follow these steps when practicing each design.

1. Prepare a fabric sandwich and mark a 4½" square on it. Divide the square into four sections. Draw diagonal lines as needed and mark any reference points.

2. Pull, secure, and trim your threads.

3. Quilt the design.

4. Check the thread tension and adjust it if needed. Also check the stitch length.

5. Practice again as needed.

Remember that you're trying to keep the majority of your stitching even and consistent. Don't succumb to the temptation to rip everything out or give up! Trust me when I tell you that all the unevenness fades away when you take a step back from the quilt.

The Oval

Draw the first two ovals using a figure-eight motion. Travel up and down the diagonal lines for the bottom of each oval.

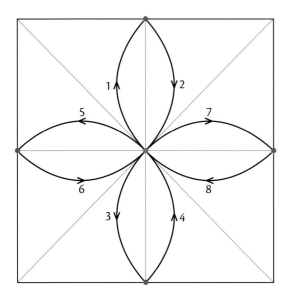

The Diagonal Oval

Try not to touch the horizontal and vertical lines with the bottom of the shape. This will keep the oval shape more defined and pointed.

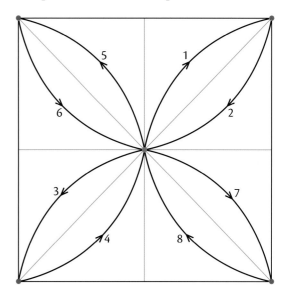

The Loop

Draw the first two loops using a figure-eight motion as you did for the Oval. Travel up and down the diagonal lines for the bottom of each loop.

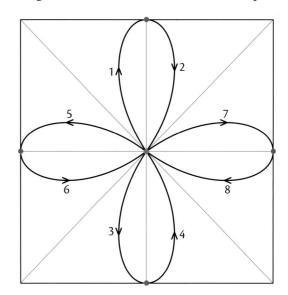

The Diagonal Loop

Mark reference points about ½" from each corner of the block. These will help you keep the widest portion of the loop consistent.

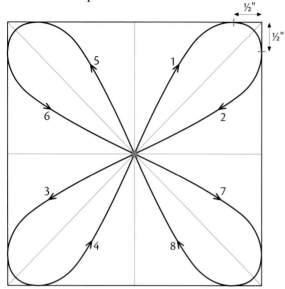

The Diagonal Lopsided Figure Eight

Draw reference points about ¾" from each corner on the diagonal lines. Use these points as places to stop and start.

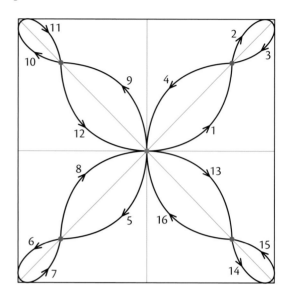

The Lopsided Figure Eight

Mark reference points on the horizontal and vertical lines about ¾" from the outside edge. Use these for stopping and starting points.

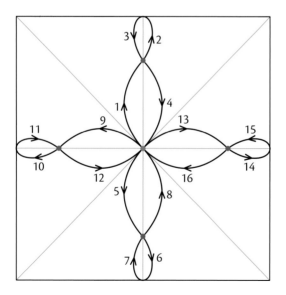

The Tulip

Draw reference points about ¾" from the outside edge on the horizontal and vertical lines and in the middle of each outside edge of the four sections. Travel up the diagonal line for the bottom of each tulip, and travel back down the diagonal line when completing each tulip section.

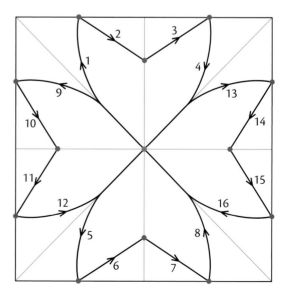

The Diagonal Tulip

Draw reference points about 1" from each corner on the diagonal lines and in the middle of each outside edge of the four sections.

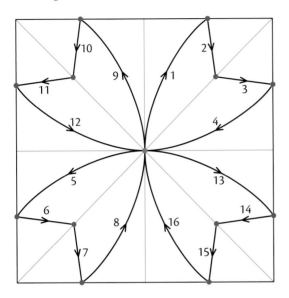

The Diagonal Heart

Follow the same instructions as for the Heart, but start at the center on the vertical line, as shown.

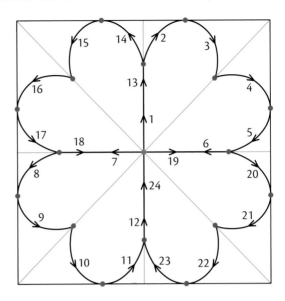

The Heart

Mark reference points as follows:

- On the horizontal and vertical lines, ¾" from the outside edge
- On the diagonal lines, 1" from the corners
- On the edge of the square, ¾" on either side of the horizontal and vertical lines

Begin at the center and travel up and down the diagonal lines to the reference points for the sides of each heart.

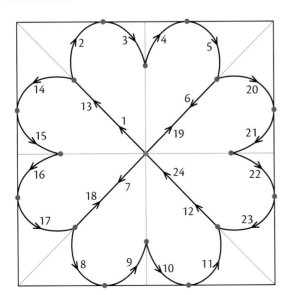

The Triangle

Mark reference points in the middle of each outside edge of the four sections. Keep your eyes focused on the outside edge reference points in order to keep your lines as straight as possible. Curve the base line of the triangle a little to make it stand out from the sides of the square.

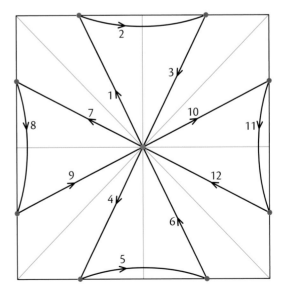

The Diagonal Triangle

Mark reference points as for The Triangle on page 25. Try to keep the base line of the triangle straight.

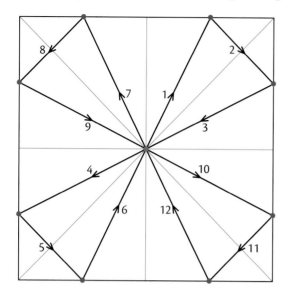

The Diagonal Diamond

Use the corners of each section as reference points. Make sure the points connect at the center and reference points.

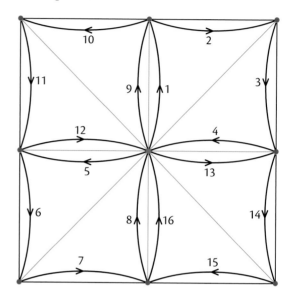

The Diamond

Mark reference points in the middle of each diagonal line. Begin at the center and make sure the points of each diamond shape connect at the reference points on the diagonals.

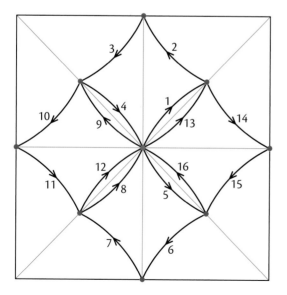

The Flower

Mark reference points in the middle of each diagonal line and about ¾" from the outside edge on the horizontal and vertical lines.

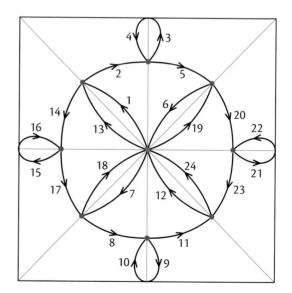

The Diagonal Flower

Mark reference points about 1" from each corner on the diagonal lines. Also use the corners of each section as reference points.

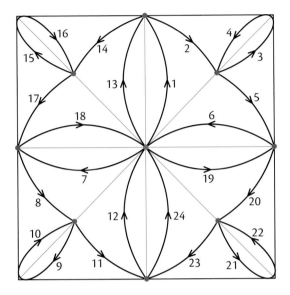

Easy Variations

There are several simple variations that can be added to some of the shapes to give you 10 more design options. Take a few minutes and try drawing each of the variations.

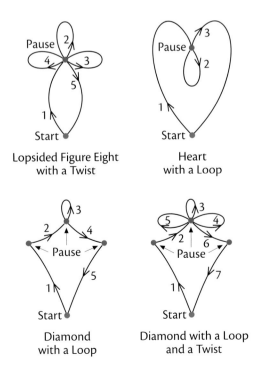

Lopsided Figure Eight
with a Twist

Heart
with a Loop

Diamond
with a Loop

Diamond with a Loop
and a Twist

Lopsided Figure Eight with a Twist

Mark reference points about ¾" from the outside edge on the horizontal and vertical lines. Use the reference points as a place to stop for the top and side loops.

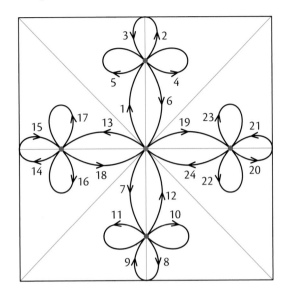

Diagonal Lopsided Figure Eight with a Twist

Mark reference points about ¾" from each corner on the diagonal lines. Use the edge of the section as the reference point for the side loops.

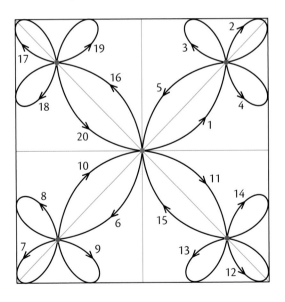

Heart with a Loop

Mark reference points as for The Heart on page 25. Add the short loop as shown. If you like this one, play around with the length of the loop for even more variations.

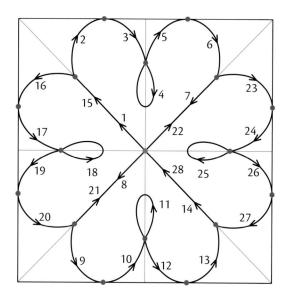

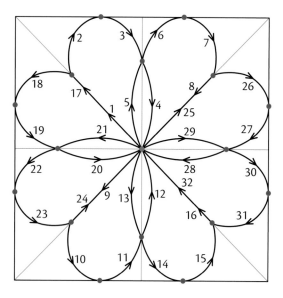

Diagonal Heart with a Loop

Mark reference points as for The Heart on page 25. Add a short loop or long loop.

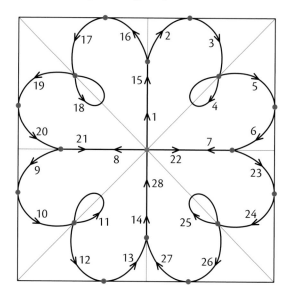

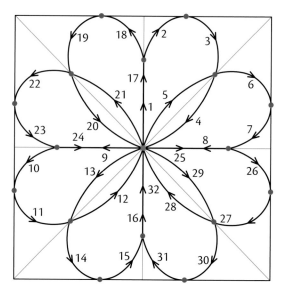

Diamond with a Loop

Varying the diamond shape by adding a loop can result in an interesting design.

Mark reference points about ¾" from the outside edge on the horizontal and vertical lines and in the middle of each diagonal line.

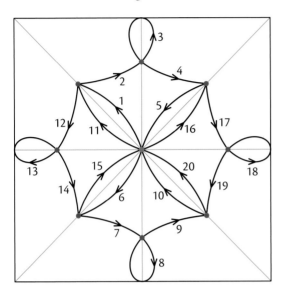

Diagonal Diamond with a Loop

Mark reference points about 1" from each corner on the diagonal lines. Also use the corners of each section as reference points.

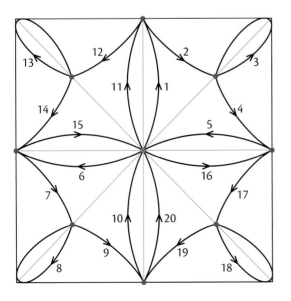

Diamond with a Loop and a Twist

Mark reference points about ¾" from the outside edge on the horizontal and vertical lines and in the middle of each diagonal line.

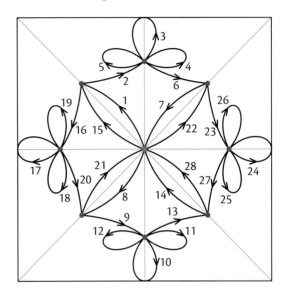

Diagonal Diamond with a Loop and a Twist

Mark reference points about ¾" from each corner on the diagonal lines. Also use the corners and edges of each section as reference points.

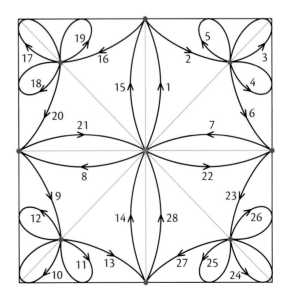

Doubled Designs

The eight shapes also look great when you double them. It gives wonderful texture to the quilt. Placing them horizontally/vertically, and then on the diagonal gives you another 16 designs for your repertoire. Give them a try and see what you think.

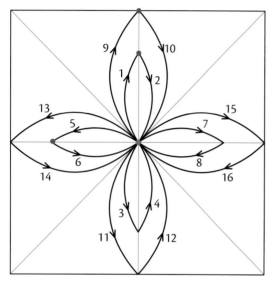

Oval—doubled

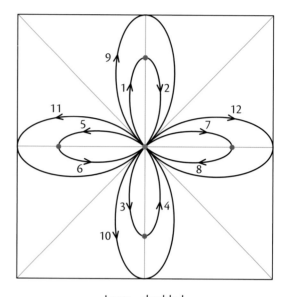

Loop—doubled

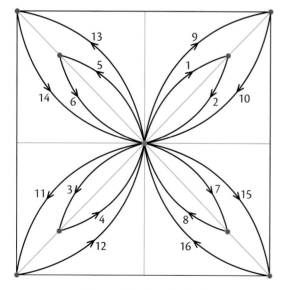

Diagonal Oval—doubled

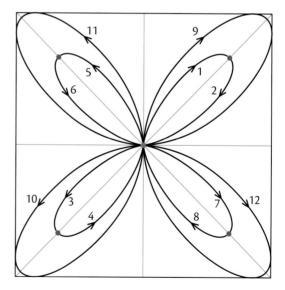

Diagonal Loop—doubled

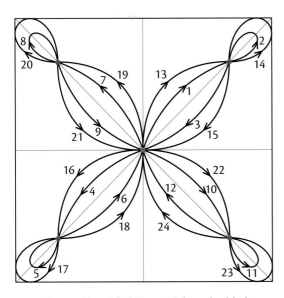

Diagonal Lopsided Figure Eight—doubled

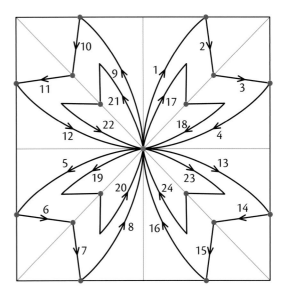

Diagonal Tulip—doubled

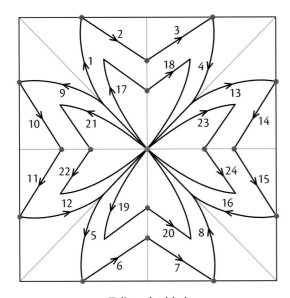

Tulip—doubled

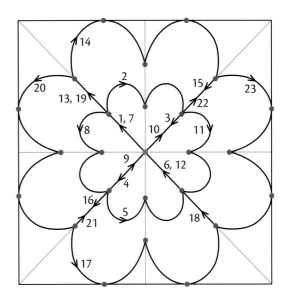

Heart—doubled

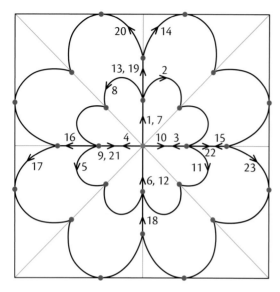

Diagonal Heart—doubled

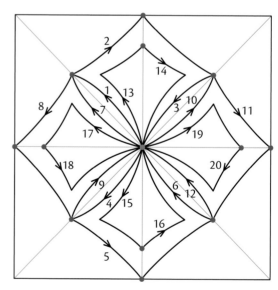

Diagonal Triangle—doubled

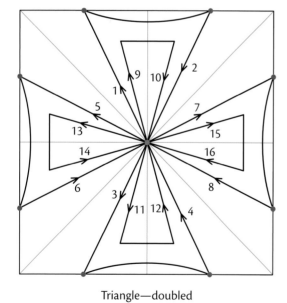

Triangle—doubled

Diamond—doubled

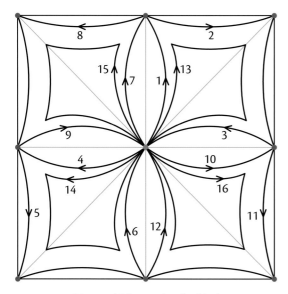

Diagonal Diamond—doubled

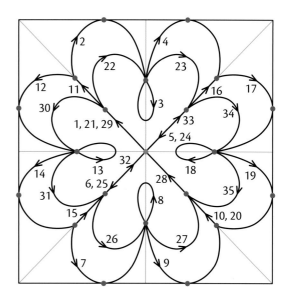

Heart with a Loop—doubled

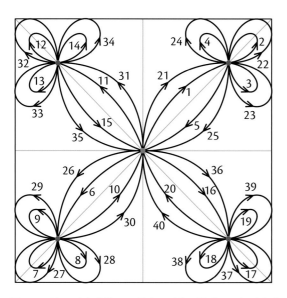

Diagonal Lopsided Figure Eight with a Twist—doubled

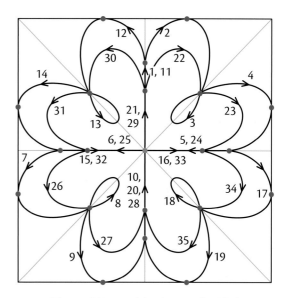

Diagonal Heart with a Loop—doubled

Summary: One Shape, Five Designs

Each basic shape can be drawn to make 5 designs. That's a total of 40 designs from eight simple shapes!

1. Draw the shape on the horizontal and vertical reference lines.
2. Draw the shape on the diagonal lines.
3. Draw the shape doubled on the horizontal and vertical reference lines.
4. Draw the shape doubled on the diagonal lines.
5. Draw the shape on the horizontal, vertical, and diagonal reference lines.

Mix-and-Match Designs

You've seen how each of the eight basic shapes and their variations produce great quilting designs. Imagine the possibilities if you start combining the shapes. The result is 144 more fantastic quilting patterns that are easy to free-motion quilt. The sheer number of designs eliminates any concern you might have as to whether or not you'll be able to find one you can quilt to your liking. Simply choose the combined design based on the shapes you feel most comfortable quilting. This way you know ahead of time you can quilt it with success!

Finding a Combined Design

To get started, first select the two shapes you want to work with. Next decide which of the shapes you want to quilt on the diagonal. Then simply look up the combined design by browsing through the designs, which are grouped together based on the shape that is quilted on the diagonal. Or you can use the handy chart on pages 36 and 37. Note that you can choose the same design for both the diagonal and the horizontal and vertical lines. The designs are provided on pages 38–73.

Using the Chart

1. Decide on the two shapes you want to use.

2. Select the shape you'll use on the diagonal. Go to the chart and find the name of that shape along the top, under the heading, "Shapes on the Diagonal."

3. Find the name of the second shape under the heading, "Shapes on the Horizontal/Vertical."

4. Follow the two columns until they intersect. The number that is listed is the page number where the design can be found.

Quilting Order

The order in which the shapes are quilted is sometimes important. This is because the first shape provides reference points for the second shape. In these cases, I've placed a star next to the shape that should be quilted first.

Marking the Designs

Follow these general guidelines to mark combined designs on your quilt top.

1. Draw a 4½" square and add the horizontal, vertical, and diagonal lines.

2. Locate the design that should be quilted *first* on pages 23–29.

3. Mark any reference points needed for the first design and draw the design following its numbered sequence.

4. Locate the design that should be quilted *second* on pages 23–29.

5. Mark any reference points needed for the second design and draw the design following its numbered sequence.

I find it helpful to re-mark any reference points shared by the two designs.

Draw Before Quilting

Even though you're working with your favorite shapes, it's still a good idea to practice drawing the combined design on paper a few times before quilting it. If you find you have some rough spots when you start quilting the design, stop and practice drawing it again. This almost always helps smooth things out.

SHAPES ON THE HORIZONTAL AND VERTICAL	SHAPES ON THE DIAGONAL						
	Oval	Loop	Lopsided Figure Eight	Tulip	Heart	Triangle	Diamond
Oval	38	41	44	47	50	53	56
Loop	38	41	44	47	50	53	56
Lopsided Figure Eight	38	41	44	47	50	53	56
Tulip	38	41	44	47	50	53	56
Heart	39	42	45	48	51	54	57
Triangle	39	42	45	48	51	54	57
Diamond	39	42	45	48	51	54	57
Flower	39	42	45	48	51	54	57
Lopsided Figure Eight with a Twist	40	43	46	49	52	55	58
Heart with a Loop	40	43	46	49	52	55	58
Diamond with a Loop	40	43	46	49	52	55	58
Diamond with a Loop and a Twist	40	43	46	49	52	55	58

SHAPES ON THE DIAGONAL					
Flower	Lopsided Figure Eight with a Twist	Heart with a Loop	Diamond with a Loop	Diamond with a Loop and a Twist	SHAPES ON THE HORIZONTAL AND VERTICAL
59	62	65	68	71	Oval
59	62	65	68	71	Loop
59	62	65	68	71	Lopsided Figure Eight
59	62	65	68	71	Tulip
60	63	66	69	72	Heart
60	63	66	69	72	Triangle
60	63	66	69	72	Diamond
60	63	66	69	72	Flower
61	64	67	70	73	Lopsided Figure Eight with a Twist
61	64	67	70	73	Heart with a Loop
61	64	67	70	73	Diamond with a Loop
61	64	67	70	73	Diamond with a Loop and a Twist

D–Oval
HV–Oval ★

D–Oval
HV–Lopsided Figure Eight ★

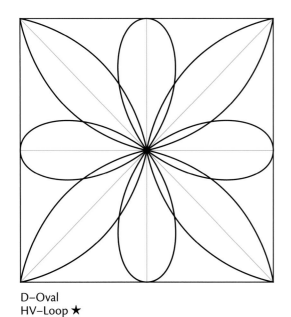

D–Oval
HV–Loop ★

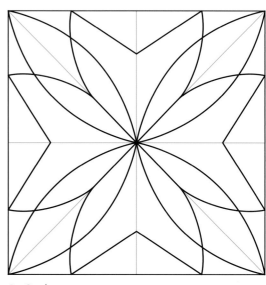

D–Oval
HV–Tulip ★

Key for Combined Designs

D = Diagonal design   HV = Horizontal and vertical design   ★ Indicates design to be quilted first

Note: Individual designs are found on pages 23–29.

D–Oval
HV–Heart ★

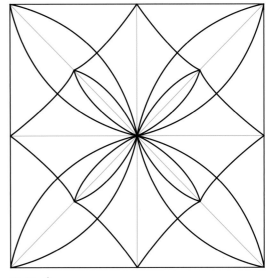

D–Oval
HV–Diamond ★

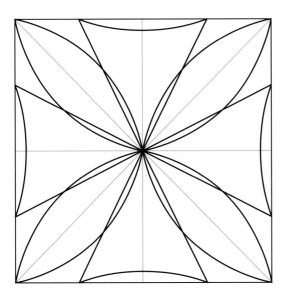

D–Oval
HV–Triangle ★

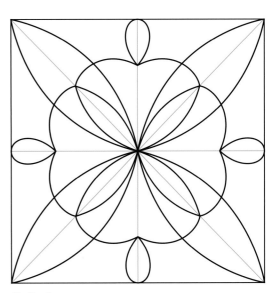

D–Oval
HV–Flower ★

D–Oval
HV–Lopsided Figure Eight with a Twist ★

D–Oval
HV–Diamond with a Loop ★

D–Oval
HV–Heart with a Loop ★

D–Oval
HV–Diamond with a Loop and a Twist ★

Key for Combined Designs

D = Diagonal design   HV = Horizontal and vertical design   ★ Indicates design to be quilted first

Note: Individual designs are found on pages 23–29.

D–Loop
HV–Oval ★

D–Loop
HV–Lopsided Figure Eight ★

D–Loop
HV–Loop ★

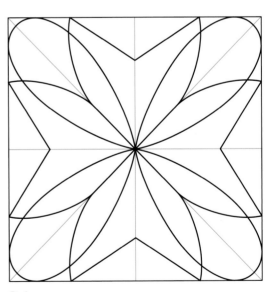

D–Loop
HV–Tulip ★

D–Loop
HV–Heart ★

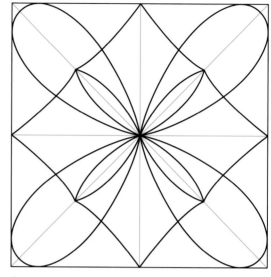

D–Loop
HV–Diamond ★

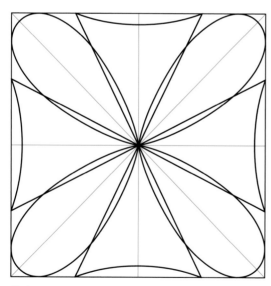

D–Loop
HV–Triangle ★

D–Loop
HV–Flower ★

Key for Combined Designs

D = Diagonal design   HV = Horizontal and vertical design   ★ Indicates design to be quilted first
Note: Individual designs are found on pages 23–29.

D–Loop
HV–Lopsided Figure Eight with a Twist ★

D–Loop
HV–Diamond with a Loop ★

D–Loop
HV–Heart with a Loop ★

D–Loop
HV–Diamond with a Loop and a Twist ★

D–Lopsided Figure Eight
HV–Oval ★

D–Lopsided Figure Eight
HV–Lopsided Figure Eight ★

D–Lopsided Figure Eight
HV–Loop ★

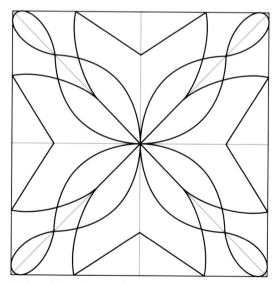

D–Lopsided Figure Eight
HV–Tulip ★

Key for Combined Designs

D = Diagonal design   HV = Horizontal and vertical design   ★ Indicates design to be quilted first

Note: Individual designs are found on pages 23–29.

D–Lopsided Figure Eight
HV–Heart ★

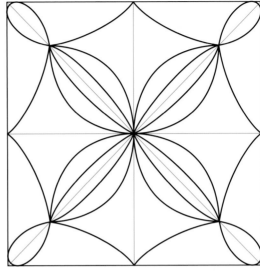

D–Lopsided Figure Eight
HV–Diamond ★

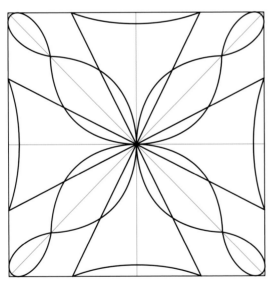

D–Lopsided Figure Eight
HV–Triangle ★

D–Lopsided Figure Eight
HV–Flower ★

D–Lopsided Figure Eight
HV–Lopsided Figure Eight with a Twist ★

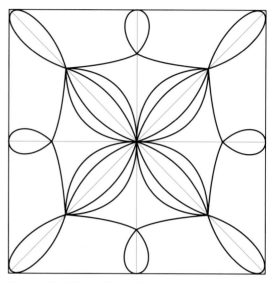

D–Lopsided Figure Eight ★
HV–Diamond with a Loop

D–Lopsided Figure Eight
HV–Heart with a Loop ★

D–Lopsided Figure Eight ★
HV–Diamond with a Loop and a Twist

Key for Combined Designs

D = Diagonal design   HV = Horizontal and vertical design   ★ Indicates design to be quilted first

Note: Individual designs are found on pages 23–29.

D–Tulip ★
HV–Oval

D–Tulip ★
HV–Lopsided Figure Eight

D–Tulip ★
HV–Loop

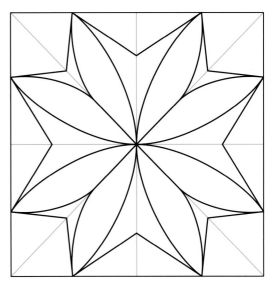

D–Tulip ★
HV–Tulip

D–Tulip ★
HV–Heart

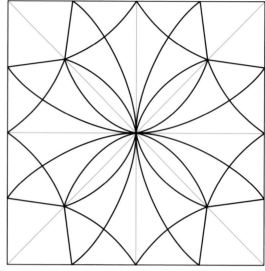

D–Tulip ★
HV–Diamond

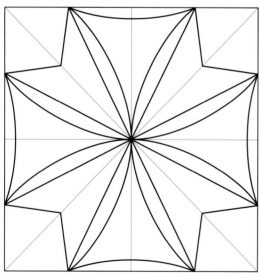

D–Tulip ★
HV–Triangle

D–Tulip ★
HV–Flower

Key for Combined Designs

D = Diagonal design   HV = Horizontal and vertical design   ★ Indicates design to be quilted first

Note: Individual designs are found on pages 23–29.

D–Tulip ★
HV–Lopsided Figure Eight with a Twist

D–Tulip ★
HV–Diamond with a Loop

D–Tulip ★
HV–Heart with a Loop

D–Tulip ★
HV–Diamond with a Loop and a Twist

D–Heart ★
HV–Oval

D–Heart ★
HV–Lopsided Figure Eight

D–Heart ★
HV–Loop

D–Heart
HV–Tulip ★

Key for Combined Designs

D = Diagonal design   HV = Horizontal and vertical design   ★ Indicates design to be quilted first

Note: Individual designs are found on pages 23–29.

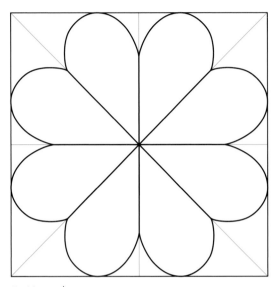

D–Heart ★
HV–Heart

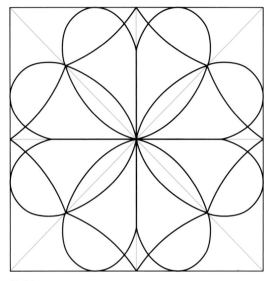

D–Heart
HV–Diamond ★

D–Heart
HV–Triangle ★

D–Heart
HV–Flower ★

D–Heart
HV–Lopsided Figure Eight with a Twist ★

D–Heart
HV–Diamond with a Loop ★

D–Heart
HV–Heart with a Loop ★

D–Heart
HV–Diamond with a Loop and a Twist ★

Key for Combined Designs

D = Diagonal design   HV = Horizontal and vertical design   ★ Indicates design to be quilted first

Note: Individual designs are found on pages 23–29.

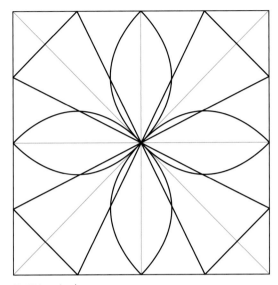

D–Triangle ★
HV–Oval

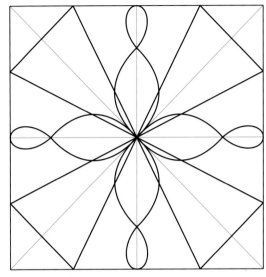

D–Triangle ★
HV–Lopsided Figure Eight

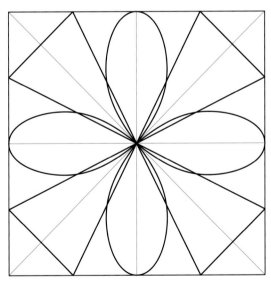

D–Triangle ★
HV–Loop

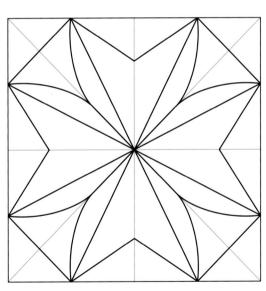

D–Triangle
HV–Tulip ★

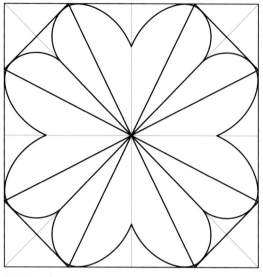

D–Triangle
HV–Heart ★

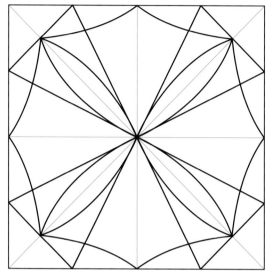

D–Triangle ★
HV–Diamond

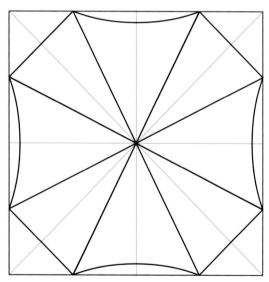

D–Triangle
HV–Triangle ★

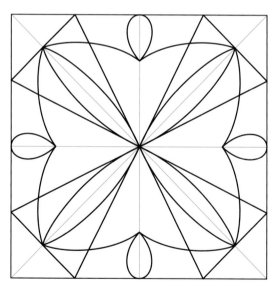

D–Triangle ★
HV–Flower

Key for Combined Designs

D = Diagonal design   HV = Horizontal and vertical design   ★ Indicates design to be quilted first

Note: Individual designs are found on pages 23–29.

D–Triangle ★
HV–Lopsided Figure Eight with a Twist

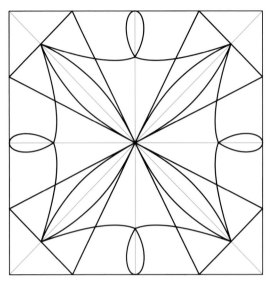

D–Triangle ★
HV–Diamond with a Loop

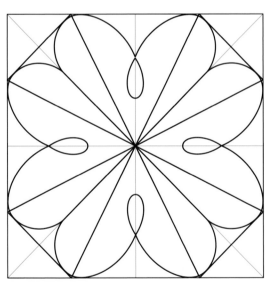

D–Triangle
HV–Heart with a Loop ★

D–Triangle ★
HV–Diamond with a Loop and a Twist

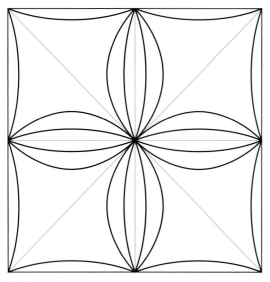

D–Diamond
HV–Oval ★

D–Diamond
HV–Lopsided Figure Eight ★

D–Diamond
HV–Loop ★

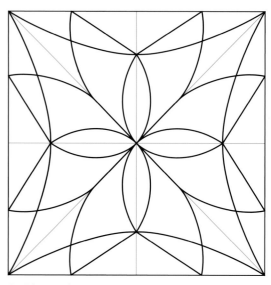

D–Diamond
HV–Tulip ★

Key for Combined Designs

D = Diagonal design   HV = Horizontal and vertical design   ★ Indicates design to be quilted first

Note: Individual designs are found on pages 23–29.

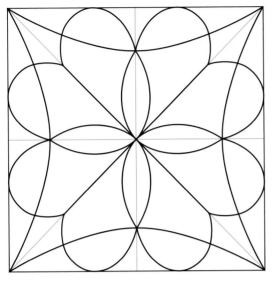

D–Diamond
HV–Heart ★

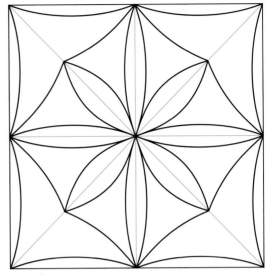

D–Diamond
HV–Diamond ★

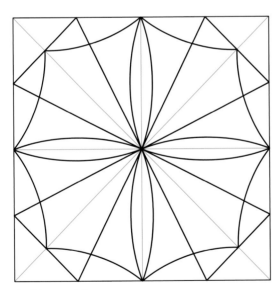

D–Diamond ★
HV–Triangle

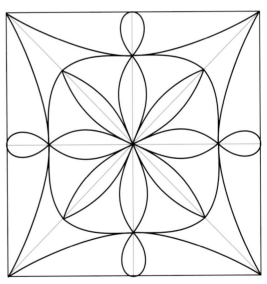

D–Diamond
HV–Flower ★

D–Diamond
HV–Lopsided Figure Eight with a Twist ★

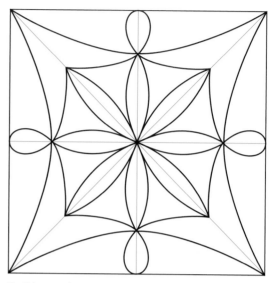

D–Diamond
HV–Diamond with a Loop ★

D–Diamond
HV–Heart with a Loop ★

D–Diamond
HV–Diamond with a Loop and a Twist ★

Key for Combined Designs

D = Diagonal design   HV = Horizontal and vertical design   ★ Indicates design to be quilted first
Note: Individual designs are found on pages 23–29.

D–Flower
HV–Oval ★

D–Flower
HV–Lopsided Figure Eight ★

D–Flower
HV–Loop ★

D–Flower
HV–Tulip ★

D–Flower
HV–Heart ★

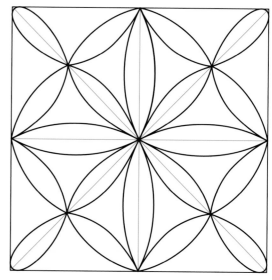

D–Flower
HV–Diamond ★

D–Flower
HV–Triangle ★

D–Flower
HV–Flower ★

Key for Combined Designs

D = Diagonal design   HV = Horizontal and vertical design   ★ Indicates design to be quilted first

Note: Individual designs are found on pages 23–29.

D–Flower
HV–Lopsided Figure Eight with a Twist ★

D–Flower
HV–Diamond with a Loop ★

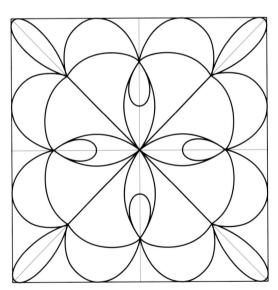

D–Flower
HV–Heart with a Loop ★

D–Flower
HV–Diamond with a Loop and a Twist ★

D–Lopsided Figure Eight with a Twist
HV–Oval ★

D–Lopsided Figure Eight with a Twist
HV–Lopsided Figure Eight ★

D–Lopsided Figure Eight with a Twist
HV–Loop ★

D–Lopsided Figure Eight with a Twist
HV–Tulip ★

Key for Combined Designs

D = Diagonal design   HV = Horizontal and vertical design   ★ Indicates design to be quilted first

Note: Individual designs are found on pages 23–29.

D–Lopsided Figure Eight with a Twist
HV–Heart ★

D–Lopsided Figure Eight with a Twist ★
HV–Diamond

D–Lopsided Figure Eight with a Twist
HV–Triangle ★

D–Lopsided Figure Eight with a Twist
HV–Flower ★

D–Lopsided Figure Eight with a Twist
HV–Lopsided Figure Eight with a Twist ★

D–Lopsided Figure Eight with a Twist ★
HV–Diamond with a Loop

D–Lopsided Figure Eight with a Twist
HV–Heart with a Loop ★

D–Lopsided Figure Eight with a Twist ★
HV–Diamond with a Loop and a Twist

Key for Combined Designs

D = Diagonal design   HV = Horizontal and vertical design   ★ Indicates design to be quilted first

Note: Individual designs are found on pages 23–29.

D–Heart with a Loop ★
HV–Oval

D–Heart with a Loop ★
HV–Lopsided Figure Eight

D–Heart with a Loop ★
HV–Loop

D–Heart with a Loop
HV–Tulip ★

D–Heart with a Loop
HV–Heart ★

D–Heart with a Loop ★
HV–Diamond

D–Heart with a Loop
HV–Triangle ★

D–Heart with a Loop ★
HV–Flower

Key for Combined Designs

D = Diagonal design   HV = Horizontal and vertical design   ★ Indicates design to be quilted first

Note: Individual designs are found on pages 23–29.

D–Heart with a Loop
HV–Lopsided Figure Eight with a Twist ★

D–Heart with a Loop ★
HV–Diamond with a Loop

D–Heart with a Loop
HV–Heart with a Loop ★

D–Heart with a Loop ★
HV–Diamond with a Loop and a Twist

D–Diamond with a Loop
HV–Oval ★

D–Diamond with a Loop
HV–Lopsided Figure Eight ★

D–Diamond with a Loop
HV–Loop ★

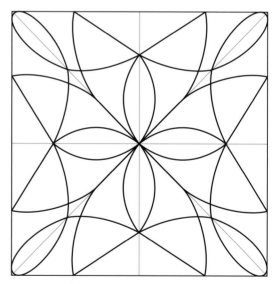

D–Diamond with a Loop
HV–Tulip ★

Key for Combined Designs

D = Diagonal design   HV = Horizontal and vertical design   ★ Indicates design to be quilted first

Note: Individual designs are found on pages 23–29.

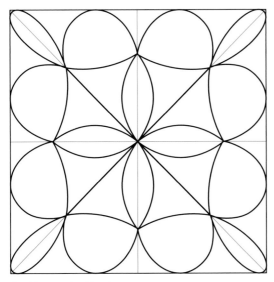

D–Diamond with a Loop
HV–Heart ★

D–Diamond with a Loop ★
HV–Diamond

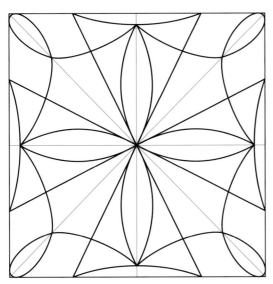

D–Diamond with a Loop
HV–Triangle ★

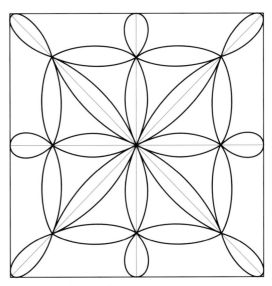

D–Diamond with a Loop
HV–Flower ★

D–Diamond with a Loop
HV–Lopsided Figure Eight with a Twist ★

D–Diamond with a Loop
HV–Diamond with a Loop ★

D–Diamond with a Loop
HV–Heart with a Loop ★

D–Diamond with a Loop
HV–Diamond with a Loop and a Twist ★

Key for Combined Designs

D = Diagonal design   HV = Horizontal and vertical design   ★ Indicates design to be quilted first

Note: Individual designs are found on pages 23–29.

D–Diamond with a Loop and a Twist
HV–Oval ★

D–Diamond with a Loop and a Twist
HV–Lopsided Figure Eight ★

D–Diamond with a Loop and a Twist
HV–Loop ★

D–Diamond with a Loop and a Twist
HV–Tulip ★

D–Diamond with a Loop and a Twist
HV–Heart ★

D–Diamond with a Loop and a Twist ★
HV–Diamond

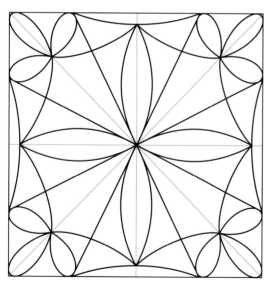

D–Diamond with a Loop and a Twist
HV–Triangle ★

D–Diamond with a Loop and a Twist ★
HV–Flower

Key for Combined Designs

D = Diagonal design   HV = Horizontal and vertical design   ★ Indicates design to be quilted first

Note: Individual designs are found on pages 23–29.

D–Diamond with a Loop and a Twist
HV–Lopsided Figure Eight with a Twist ★

D–Diamond with a Loop and a Twist ★
HV–Diamond with a Loop

D–Diamond with a Loop and a Twist
HV–Heart with a Loop ★

D–Diamond with a Loop and a Twist
HV–Diamond with a Loop and a Twist ★

What and Where to Quilt

Deciding how to quilt your finished quilt top can seem overwhelming. I take a systematic approach that I believe makes the whole process easier. I start by deciding where I want to put the quilting designs. I do this by shifting my focus from looking at the whole quilt top to studying the individual quilt blocks.

Break the Block into Smaller Sections

Quilting in smaller 4½"-square sections is still our primary focus when deciding where to put the design. It's the first thing that has to be considered when studying the individual quilt block. Since very few finished quilt blocks are this small, you need an easy way to break the block down into a grid of 4½" square or smaller sections or shapes. Once it's broken down, any of the designs can be used in it regardless of its overall size. There are several ways to accomplish this.

Block units. A pieced quilt block is typically constructed in units. The units are sewn into rows, and the rows are sewn together to form a block. The individual units form a grid. The most commonly used grids in patchwork are the nine-patch and four-patch grids. Let's say the finished size of the block is 12" square. It's too big to quilt with one overall design. However, it can easily be broken down into a grid using the block units. As shown below, each of the units is 4" square. They fit perfectly within our smaller quilting space. You now have the quilt block broken into smaller, more manageable quilting areas and can easily quilt any one of the designs in some or all of the units.

Block seam lines. Blocks can also be broken into a grid of smaller quilting sections by using its seam lines. I use this method when I'm working with blocks such as the Log Cabin, which is constructed more with long strips than square units. Simply use some type of temporary fabric-marking tool (my favorite, of course, is the white Chaco

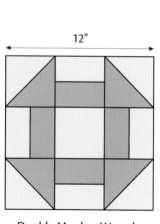

Double Monkey Wrench.
Nine-patch grid.

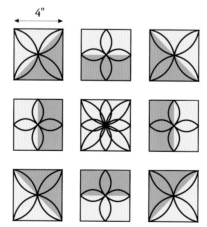

Shape: Oval

Liner) to continue the seam lines out to the edge of the block. The connected lines produce a grid that can easily be divided into smaller quilting sections.

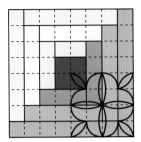

Shape: Basic flower
——— Seam line
- - - - Drawn lines

Surrounding block seam lines. You can also divide a block into a grid of smaller quilting sections by using the seams of the surrounding blocks. This can be very useful when your quilt has a plain alternate block. Let's say our quilt is made up of two different 7½" square blocks, the Ohio Star block and a plain block. The blocks are too big to quilt as a whole, but you can break the Ohio Star block down into a nine-patch grid with sections that are 2½" square.

You can break the plain block into the same nine-patch grid by using the seam lines from the Ohio Star block. Simply extend the lines created by the seams across the plain block. You now have both quilt blocks divided into a grid of manageable quilting sections and can quilt them as desired.

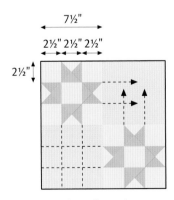

Draw lines from the seams
to the edges of the block.

This same method can be used when working with a block such as the Rail Fence that only has seam lines going in one direction.

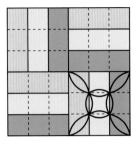

Shape: Basic oval
——— Seam line
- - - - Drawn lines

Block shapes. A quilt block will usually break down into some combination of squares, rectangles, and triangles. You can also use these shapes to create smaller more manageable quilting sections.

Square   Rectangle

Half-square   Quarter-square
triangle unit   triangle unit

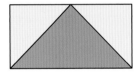

Flying geese

Three-triangle   Square in
unit   a square

As an example, the Square in a Square block consists of a square and four triangles. Let's say the finished block is 7" square and too large to quilt as a whole; however, the size of each shape falls within our smaller quilting area. You could now quilt a design in the center square and in each of the triangles.

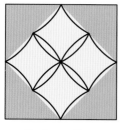

Design quilted
in the square

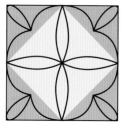

Design quilted
in each triangle shape

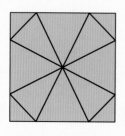

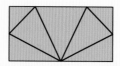

Shape: Flower

Start with a Square

Remember that rectangles and triangles can simply be half of a square. Draw the design in a square, and then divide it in half to see how it will fit into the rectangle or triangle.

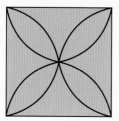

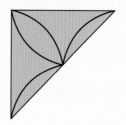

Fitting Strategies

It's so much easier to keep a quilting design smooth and consistent when no part of the design is longer than 2½". However, the dimensions of your quilting space may not always be this small. There are ways to compensate for this and keep your designs a manageable size.

Let's say you're working with a 5" block; you have marked the horizontal, vertical, and diagonal reference lines. On the horizontal and vertical lines, the distance from the center of the block out to the edge of the block measures 2½". You can use any of the designs in this location. However, the distance along the diagonal measures 3½". This is longer than our ideal quilting area.

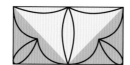
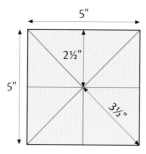

You can try breaking the space into smaller segments or use a quilting design that has a stopping point in it. An example would be the Lopsided Figure Eight. Draw the first loop so that it is about 2½" long, pause, and reposition your hands if necessary, and then finish the final loop.

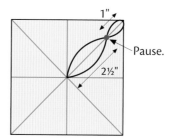

There are times when you just can't reduce the size of the area you need to quilt down to 2½" or use a design with a stopping point. The area can still be quilted, but be warned that it's harder to keep the designs consistent. The best thing to do to reduce any wobbliness is to keep the quilting close to the reference lines.

Secondary Patterns

When you're breaking a quilt block down by shapes, consider any shapes formed at the intersections of surrounding blocks as well. These are the secondary patterns. It usually looks better when these areas are quilted with one complete design instead of individual shapes. This helps eliminate block lines and adds dimension to the quilt.

Secondary shapes formed
at block intersections

To Quilt or Not to Quilt

You now have your quilt block broken down into either a grid of smaller sections or shapes. You could quilt the entire quilt top by filling each section with any one of the designs in this book. It looks great and is often how I choose to quilt. However, sometimes it's nice to leave some of the sections or shapes unquilted. I personally love the extra texture the unquilted area adds. Just be sure to keep the quilting balanced; any unquilted sections should be about the same size as the quilted sections. As a general rule, I don't leave any area larger than 4" unquilted. Check the requirements of your batting for guidelines as well.

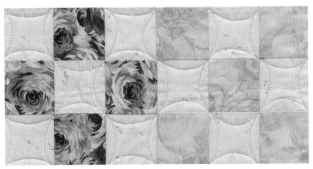

Quilted and unquilted sections of Nine-Patch quilt.

There are two factors I consider when deciding whether or not to quilt an area. First is the fabric. If you have a busy focus fabric, don't spend your creative energies quilting in that section. The quilting won't show up. Just use a light design, and then highlight the quilting in the next area where it will really show.

The second way to narrow down the areas you quilt is to consider how heavily an area is pieced, and how thick the seams are. Areas where several seam allowances overlap are difficult to stitch evenly. The needle tends to get stuck in the seams, and you end up with areas of very tiny stitches where the needle caught and some very large stitches where the needle suddenly released. I find it helpful to slow down my quilting when I get to these seams and "walk" the needle over the area. Keep the designs to a minimum in these areas if you have to quilt them at all.

The Quilting Design

You're now ready to choose the quilting design. The nice thing about these designs is they look good on any type of quilt, traditional or contemporary. This allows you to select your designs based more on your comfort level with the different shapes than on the style or feel of the quilt. Take a look through the shapes and the designs with your quilt top in mind and see which one catches your eye. Draw the design a few times to make sure you're comfortable with it, and then "audition" it on the quilt.

Limit the Number of Shapes

A couple of shapes can usually do the job nicely. Reusing the designs in different areas of the quilt rather than adding in more gives the quilting a more consistent look. I probably wouldn't use more than three shapes on a quilt.

Audition the Design

I like to have an idea of how a design will look in a section of the quilt before I commit to stitching it. There are several ways to do this. My favorite is to actually draw it on the quilt with a white Chaco Liner. You can also get an idea for how a design will look by making a copy of the quilt block, either from the quilt itself or from the pattern, and sketching out the shapes. You can also simply sketch the block on graph paper, and then play with the designs.

1. Choose a couple of your favorite shapes or combined designs, the ones you feel most confident drawing and quilting.

2. Select the area of the quilt block where you would like to try the design.

3. Draw in reference lines (horizontal, vertical, and diagonal lines) and any needed reference points with your Chaco Liner or temporary marking tool. Try to use the block seam lines as reference lines whenever possible.

4. Draw the design in the space. Watch to see if the design fills the space evenly and has a natural flow to it. Your goal is to be able to move easily from one area to the next.

5. Make changes as needed until you're satisfied with the look.

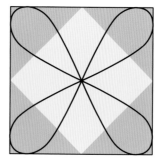

Loops look awkward in the triangular areas of the block.

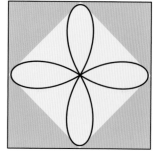

Loops are more balanced.

Design is interesting, but it might be too busy in a small block.

Design is more evenly distributed in the block.

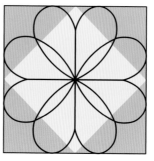

The fit of the design is good, but the sides of the heart could be improved.

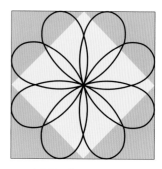

Adding loops creates a pleasing design.

Continuous Free-Motion Quilting of the Design

It's often possible to make the quilting of the designs in each section continuous, meaning you don't have to stop and trim the threads after each design. It's something to watch for when auditioning your designs in the quilt block. The key is to watch for places where designs and/or shapes from two sections meet at a seam line. These designs have the potential to be connected for continuous free-motion quilting if you can easily travel over the seam and hide the stitches connecting them. I sometimes even change a shape I'm using if another shape would make the quilting more continuous.

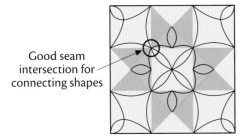

Good seam intersection for connecting shapes

Design Connectors

I tend to use the Oval shape more than the Loop shape because it's easier to connect designs for continuous quilting when the shapes meet at a point. You can easily stop at a point to hide your stitches. I also change the loops of a shape like the Diamond with a Loop and a Twist to ovals when connecting them to another design. I call these "design connectors."

Diamond with a Loop and a Twist   Revised design

Another design connector I use is a half oval or an arc. I call the half-oval shape a "hop" because it allows me to connect designs for continuous quilting by "hopping" from one section to another. I add hops to a design during the audition process when I need a way to connect the shapes.

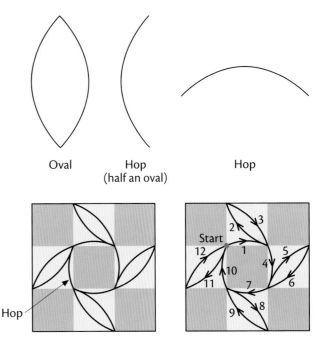

Oval   Hop (half an oval)   Hop

Hop

Stippling can also be used as a design connector. It adds great texture to the block and can be especially helpful when you need a way to move around the outside of the block in an attempt to make the quilting more continuous. Don't be afraid to add it to the mix!

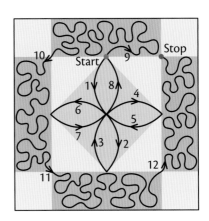

Change the Starting Point

Another way to make the quilting more continuous is to change the starting point and/or the order in which the design is quilted. Up to this point, you've practiced by starting your design in the center and completing each shape before quilting the rest of the block. For more continuous stitching, start quilting at one of the seam intersections where the two designs or shapes connect. Quilt a half or a quarter of the first shape to get back to the center of the block; then complete the rest of the design by working your way around the block. You'll finish the design by quilting the other half of the first shape.

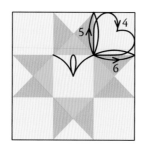

You can continuously quilt the design by changing your starting point and altering the order you quilt the designs.

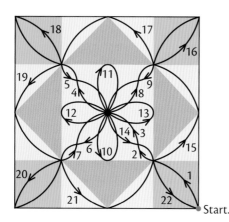

Continuous Quilting Several Blocks

Changing the starting point and the order in which you quilt the design will also help you to continuously quilt several blocks at a time. Look for an area where the designs from four adjacent blocks meet. Then quilt half the shapes needed to get to the center design of one block; quilt the rest of the design within the block. After you complete the center, look to see if there are additional elements of the design that still need to be finished. If there are, work your way around the block, with hops if needed, until the rest of the block is quilted and you're back to where you started. Finish the first half shape and start the process again with the next block.

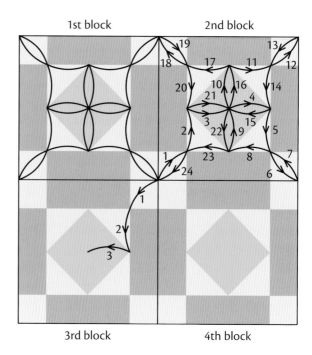

I love to quilt continuously, but with these designs I have found it best to only connect four blocks at a time. Technically you could do more, but it would really spread out your quilting and I think it tends to get confusing. If at first you find it too confusing to try and connect any of the designs, then don't worry about it. There is nothing wrong with quilting one design at a time. It doesn't make a difference to the look of the design whether it is quilted continuously or not.

Also, don't get discouraged if you get lost a few times as you try to make the quilting more continuous. It still happens to me occasionally. If you find yourself in this situation, just finish what you can, secure and trim your threads, and start again where you need to. It's not a big deal.

Putting It All Together

At first glance, the process of choosing designs and connecting them for continuous quilting may look intimidating. It's really not that bad. Just take a few minutes to map out your design and practice the "route" until you're comfortable with it. Remember, the worst thing that can happen is you don't connect the designs and have to stop your quilting a few more times. Here's a summary of the process:

1. Break the block into a grid or shapes.
2. Decide on the shapes and designs you want to use.
3. Audition the designs in the quilt block.
4. Look for points where the designs touch.
5. Change any connecting shapes from loops to ovals if needed.
6. Look to see if the designs from adjacent blocks meet at any seam intersections.
7. Determine the best starting place.
8. Add in any hops to make the design more continuous.
9. Map out the best path to follow.

Make a Map

Once I decide on the final design, I draw it on paper and number the sequence of steps. I find it very helpful to keep this map by my machine while quilting.

I like to double check how my design looks early on in the quilting. I'll stitch one or two blocks, and then stop, securing and trimming my threads. I take the quilt out from under the machine and lay it on my bed. This allows me to stand back and see how the design is developing. There are times, even after auditioning my designs, that I don't like them stitched. I have found it better to simply stop and take out the quilting before going any further. Yes, the dreaded seam ripper! Trust me, it's better to do it when you only have one or two blocks done instead of twelve. Just put on some relaxing music, get a cup of coffee or wine, and do it. It will be done before you know it.

Quilting Beyond the Blocks

My decision process for how to handle the rest of the quilt is primarily based on the fabric used in those specific areas. Once again it comes down to whether or not the quilting will show up on the fabric. When I can highlight the quilting in these areas, I try to use the same shapes from the block designs. I think repetition of the shapes gives the quilt a very polished look.

Sashing

Quilt tops are often put together with sashing separating the blocks. Plan for the quilting in these areas when you're deciding how to quilt your blocks. You can handle sashing in one of three ways:

- Leave it unquilted as a textural contrast to the quilted sections. Sashing usually isn't much wider than 2"; your quilting will still be balanced if the sashing isn't quilted.
- Stipple quilt the sashing; this would allow you to make the quilting of your blocks more continuous.
- Use the seam lines from the surrounding blocks to divide the sashing into smaller, more manageable quilting sections. This allows you to incorporate the block quilting design into the sashing.

Let's look at the Cross with a Cross block with sashing and cornerstones. I've included two examples where the seam lines were used to break the sashing into more manageable sections. In the first example, the sashing is quilted at the same time as the block. In the second example, the block is quilted first, and then the sashing is quilted continuously using hops.

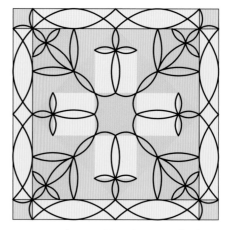

Example 2: Sashing design quilted after the block

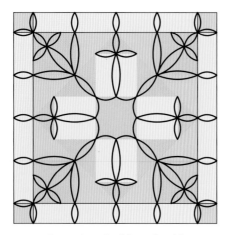

Example 1: Quilting of sashing included with overall block design

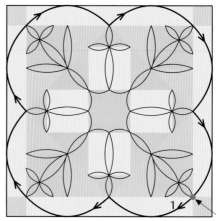

Complete the design inside the block. Stitch the first round of the sashing using hops.

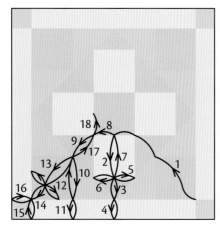

Quilt half of the first two shapes to get to the center of the design. Continue quilting in the suggested pattern.

Quilt the second part of the sashing. Move to the next quilt block and continue quilting.

Inner Borders

I handle the inner quilt borders pretty much the same as the sashing and primarily use the fabric as the determining factor as to how much quilting to do and which design to use.

For fabrics where the quilting will show, I divide the borders into manageable sections using the seam lines from the surrounding blocks or simply dividing it into sections I feel comfortable working with. I then try to incorporate some part of the block's quilting design into the border. For fabrics with a busy print, I use a meandering or stippling design or leave it unquilted, depending on the width. I think any border up to about 2½" can be left unquilted.

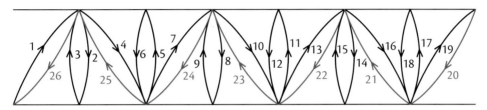

Quilt this border in two rounds, first quilting hops and ovals.
On the second pass, use hops to complete it.

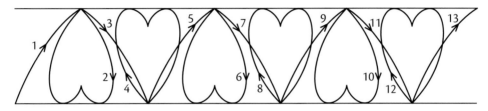

Connect alternating hearts with hops.

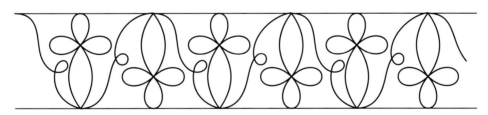

Connect designs with meandering loops or stippling.

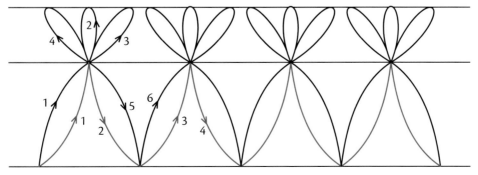

Quilt two borders at once in two passes.

Outer Borders

I don't worry about the outer borders of a quilt until I've finished quilting the center. Once I'm done with the quilt blocks and any sashing or inner borders, I lay the quilt on my bed to look at it. The first thing I consider, once again, is the border fabric. The main border fabric is generally the focus fabric for the quilt and tends to be busy. I won't spend the extra time dividing the border into smaller sections if the designs won't show up. I often meander or stipple them, incorporating one of the shapes into the meandering pattern.

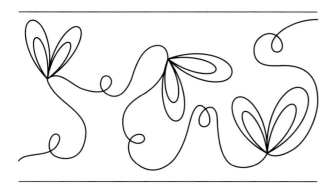

If the design will show up on the fabric, try to use the quilt blocks to mark reference points in the borders. Then include part of the block design in the border. It can really look fantastic. Continuous quilting of the borders often requires that you quilt the border in two rounds.

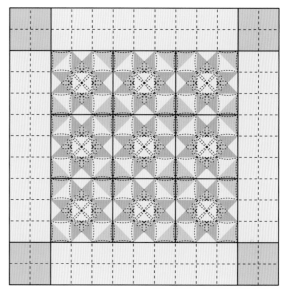

The quilt block's seam lines are drawn out into the border.

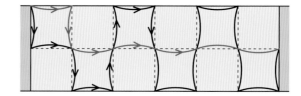

Overall look with quilting design continued into the border

Multicolor Four Patch and Plain Block Quilt, 42½" x 50½".
Finished block size: 8" x 8".

The Lopsided Figure Eight shape is quilted on the horizontal/vertical and diagonal lines in the gold blocks. The Lopsided Figure Eight and Loop combined design is quilted in the pink and Four Patch blocks. Even though the quilting designs are simple, they still provide great texture to the quilt.

Pink Four Patch Wall Hanging,
29" x 34". Finished block size:
4½" x 4½".

The Diamond and Loop combined design is used. The Loop shape gives the design a circular feel and draws the eye around the quilt.

Pink and Blue Four Patch and Plain Block Quilt, 42" x 56½".
Finished block size: 9½" x 9½".

The Oval shape is quilted on both the horizontal/vertical and diagonal lines. Even though the design is the same in each block, it looks different due to the color of the fabric it's quilted on. Half of the design is used in the partial blocks at the edge of the quilt center. This half design could also be quilted in the blue border using the seam lines as a way to divide the border into more manageable sections.

Basket Wall Hanging, 29" x 29".
Finished block size: 4½" x 4½".

The Oval shape was quilted in the Basket block with the bottom oval being longer than the others. The Diamond with a Loop shape was quilted on the diagonal in the plain block. Half of the plain block design is used to quilt the setting triangles.

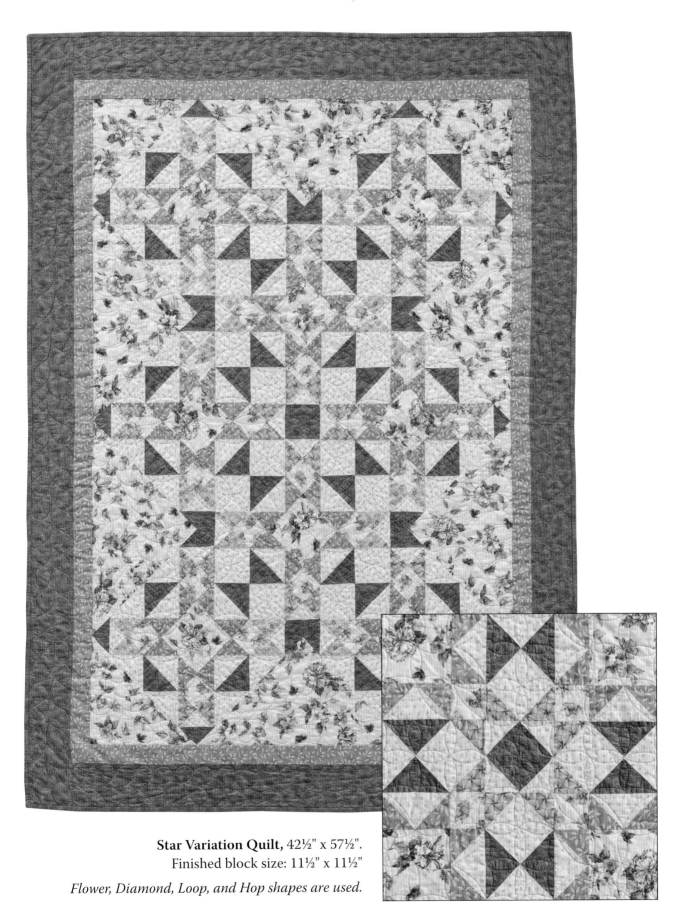

Star Variation Quilt, 42½" x 57½".
Finished block size: 11½" x 11½"

Flower, Diamond, Loop, and Hop shapes are used.

Gentleman's Fancy Variation Quilt, 69" x 69". Finished block size: 11½" x 11½".

The Diamond , Oval, and Hop shapes are used in both the main and alternate blocks but are arranged differently. The design from the alternate block is used in the border blocks; it's doubled in the light-colored block. This design was also used again in the corner block.

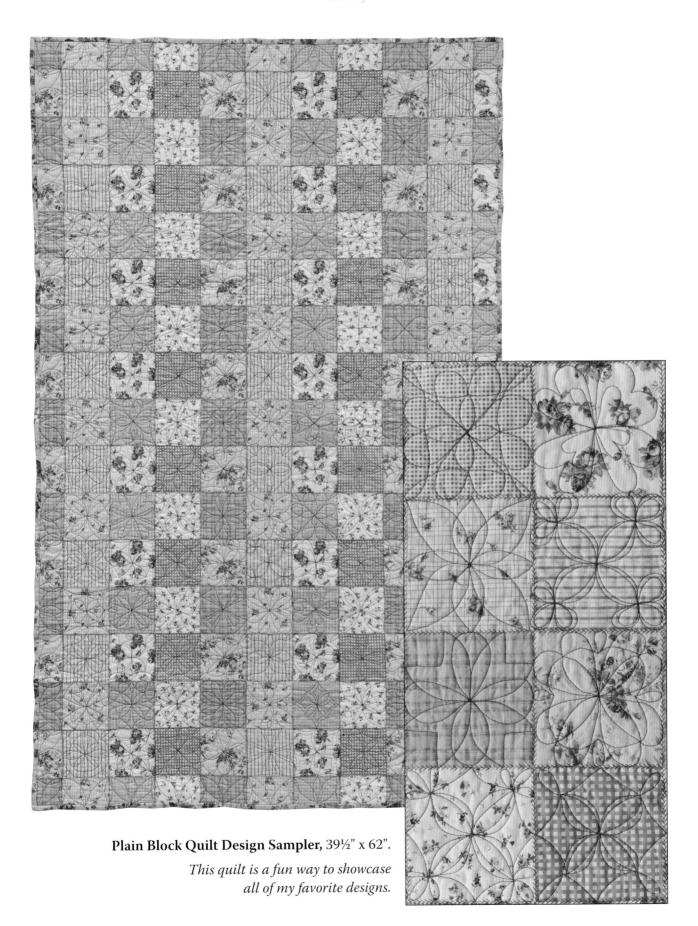

Plain Block Quilt Design Sampler, 39½" x 62".

*This quilt is a fun way to showcase
all of my favorite designs.*

Baby Sampler Quilt, 42½" x 50".
Finished block size: 4" x 4".

Using a different design in each block shows how a simple quilt can quickly be made to look extra special. The designs really pop out and make you take a second look at this little quilt. Solid-colored fabrics allow the quilting designs to be the star of the show.

Nine Patch Quilt, 50" x 64½".
Finished block size: 7" x 7".

*The Diamond shape is quilted in only
the cream colored blocks. This allows
the same thread color to be used over
the entire center of the quilt. The design
required no marking and enabled several
blocks to be quilted continuously.*

Troubleshooting

No matter how hard you try, sometimes problems do occur when free-motion quilting. In this section I've provided a short troubleshooting guide for the problems that occur most often.

Rethread the Machine

I can't tell you the number of times I've seen a problem resolved by rethreading the machine. It's probably the cause of about 90% of the problems when free-motion quilting. The key when rethreading the machine is to completely redo it. Cut the top thread and take the top thread spool all the way off the sewing machine. Put the thread back on the machine and rethread it. Next take the bobbin out of the bobbin case, and then put it back in, making sure the thread goes through the tension guide. Test the stitching to see if this has resolved the problem. If not, try it one more time. If it still isn't fixed, try one of the solutions in the troubleshooting guide.

TROUBLESHOOTING GUIDE	
Problem	*Causes and Solutions*
Skipped stitches	Dust buildup in bobbin area. A dirty bobbin case is probably the main reason your machine will start to skip stitches. Get into the habit of brushing the lint out of the bobbin case each time you run out of bobbin thread. I use a soft bristled paintbrush and go over the whole bobbin case area. After every four bobbin refills, I take off the throat plate, remove the entire bobbin case, and clean the whole area. (Check your sewing machine manual if you're not sure how to remove the bobbin case.)
	Needle is dull and needs to be replaced.
	Needle is in the wrong way.
	Needle is threaded incorrectly.
	Thread used in the top of the machine is a different weight or size than that used in the bobbin. I always use the same-weight thread in both the top of the machine and in the bobbin.
	Thread tension that is too tight can cause skipped stitches. I recommend rethreading the machine and turning the tension back to its standard setting. Then slowly start adjusting the tension, making half-step changes between each stitch test.
	Machine needs servicing. If you've tried all the items mentioned and are still having problems, your machine may need service. It's a good idea to have your machine serviced at least once a year.

TROUBLESHOOTING GUIDE	
Problem	*Causes and Solutions*
Broken needles	Pulling the quilt or moving it too quickly can cause a needle to break. This usually happens when you're not stopping enough during your quilting and/or you're trying to quilt an area larger than 4½" square.
	Incorrect needle. Using the wrong type of needle can cause it to break. Try a quilting needle; it has a very sharp point and a more tapered shaft to help it go through all the layers of the quilt. Also try a jeans needle; it has an extra strong shaft that can help prevent breaking.
Thread nest on the back of the quilt	Bobbin thread was not pulled up to the top of the quilt before free-motion quilting.
	Bobbin was wound unevenly. A correctly wound bobbin should feel smooth and firm. It has a spongy feel to it if it hasn't been wound correctly.
	Machine is not threaded correctly on top and/or in the bobbin. A thread nest usually appears when one of the threads has not gone through its tension guide. Try completely rethreading the machine.
Thread breakage or shredding	Sewing speed is too fast. Slow down.
	Thread spool position needs to be changed. Some spools of thread are meant to unwind from a vertical position. Sewing machines will often have an additional spool holder that can be attached so spools can sit upright. A thread stand can also help rectify this problem.
	Type of needle is incorrect. All sewing machine needles are not the same. They have different shafts and eyes. The type of needle to use is dependent upon the type of fabric and thread you are using. This is especially true when dealing with metallic thread. A metallic needle has a larger eye to accommodate the thread and help prevent it from shredding.
	Upper tension is too tight. Try loosening the top thread tension by half steps. Make sure you watch what happens to the thread tension on the back of the quilt. If the thread starts to lie on the back of the quilt and the thread is still breaking, you might need to try a heavier thread. Thread with a low-weight number is actually thicker and stronger than thread with a high-weight number. Basic sewing thread has a weight of about 60; the weight of most quilting thread is in the 30 to 40 range.
	Poor-quality or old thread.
	Dust buildup in bobbin area.
	Thread used in the top of the machine differs from that used in the bobbin. Use the same-weight thread in both.
	Machine is threaded incorrectly.

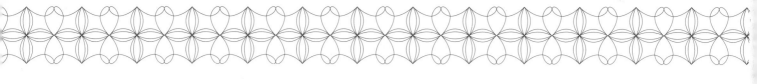

About the Author

Eva started quilting in 1999 while living in Australia. It wasn't until she moved back to the States in 2002 that she took her first free-motion quilting class. For the next several years she bought whatever books she could find on the subject and took any additional classes she could find. In 2003 she started working in a quilt store and soon found herself teaching classes on free-motion quilting. Her quilting on store samples was noticed, and a small quilting business slowly emerged. It was during her time as a professional quilter that she started to develop and teach free-motion quilting designs that could be successfully quilted on a domestic sewing machine, which she used in her business instead of a long-arm quilting machine. Her goal was to develop designs that the everyday quilter, like herself, could consistently quilt without spending a lot of time practicing and marking the quilt. Those design ideas are the foundation for her free-motion quilting classes and this book. Her favorite phrase is "You can do it!" and she uses it when teaching classes or sharing ideas with other quilters on free-motion quilting designs. She truly believes that everyone who wants to can free-motion quilt and achieve good results. Eva continues to dream up new designs for free-motion quilting in addition to teaching and quilting professionally.